Praise for
Risk
by Kenny Luck

"I've always been an adrenaline junkie, so *Risk* instantly appealed to me. This book goes beyond the interesting and engaging *descriptive stories* to provide much needed *prescriptive insight* to enable men to live more boldly and powerfully. If you're up for being challenged in significant ways, read this book."

—Mark Sanborn, president of Sanborn and Associates Inc. and author of *The Fred Factor: How Passion in Your Work and Life Can Turn the Ordinary into the Extraordinary*

"Shocking are the Scripture's stories of men that took risks! So are the modern-day accounts of men changing the world for God by taking risks. And then there's you... Are you risking it? This is a man's book for men—men of God ready to rip into the ends of the age. Dive into *Risk!*"

—Dr. Wayne Cordeiro, senior pastor of New Hope Christian Fellowship Oahu and author of *Doing Church as a Team* and *Culture Shift*

"*Risk* is a book for men. It challenges us to faith, courage, and commitment. Kenny Luck tells the inspiring stories of men who risked everything to follow God. Don't miss this exciting and riveting challenge. It will stir your soul to action."

—Dr. Jerry Falwell, Liberty University in Lynchburg, Virginia

"I always want to know if the author of a book exemplifies what he has written. Kenny Luck certainly does! He has taken the risk to leave what seemed more comfortable and secure in order to follow God's call in his life. *Risk: Are You Willing to Trust God with Everything?* invites men everywhere to do the same. It is a book that is not afraid to confront the realities, to challenge the heart, and to celebrate the joy that are a part of the risk of faith."

—Tom Holladay, teaching pastor at Saddleback Church and author of *Foundations: 11 Core Truths to Build Your Life On*

"*Risk* is a must-read for any man seeking significant change in his life. This book has great depth and momentum. Kenny Luck clearly communicates the message of what it means to completely sell out to God. Thank you Kenny. I pray that all men everywhere will take the risk and trust God with everything."

—Davey Buhl, director of men's ministry at Christ Church at Grove Farm

"*Risk* is my kind of book, and Kenny Luck is my kind of guy. Jesus lived risking everything, and this book inspires you and me to live like Jesus lived and to do what Jesus did. Warning: *Risk* is for the courageous, not cowards. Be bold! Buy *Risk!* Live it!"

—Walt Kallestad, author of *Entrepreneurial Faith; A Passionate Life; The Passionate Church;* and *Turn Your Church Inside Out;* and senior pastor of Community Church of Joy in Glendale, Arizona

"Kenny brings a fresh challenge to every Christian man by stepping up and accepting the risks of speaking out for God. As a pastor, I get the joy of seeing how this message lives out weekly through our men at Saddleback Church. It's not theory, but real! Kenny's passion and calling is making a difference!"

—Doug Slaybaugh, president of Purpose Driven

"*Risk* challenges the heart of the many issues that men are dealing with today. Kenny has done a thorough job of meeting men where they are and giving us a game plan to be men of God. I highly recommend that all men read *Risk* and allow the encouragements to saturate their lives."

—Greg Surratt, senior pastor of Seacoast Church

risk
workbook

Are you willing to trust God
with everything?

kenny luck

WaterBrook
Press

RISK WORKBOOK
PUBLISHED BY WATERBROOK PRESS
12265 Oracle Boulevard, Suite 200
Colorado Springs, Colorado 80921
A division of Random House Inc.

Details in some anecdotes and stories have been changed to protect the identities of the persons involved.

ISBN 978-1-57856-991-5

Printed in the United States of America
2007

10 9 8 7 6 5 4 3 2

contents

How to Use This Workbook 1

Introduction 3

Week One: Risk Taking 7

Week Two: "Be It So" 27

Week Three: Created for Worship 45

Week Four: Getting Real 63

Week Five: Game On 81

Week Six: Godly "Gut Feel" 99

Week Seven: "Use Me" 117

Week Eight: Risk It All 135

how to use this workbook

This workbook, which is a companion to the book *Risk,* is designed to be used in three ways:

1. *Personal workbook.* If you want to grow in faith and find out what it means to risk your life for the cause of Christ, you will enjoy unpacking challenging material and applying it to your own journey as God's man. Each session in the workbook contains two sections for personal study and action: Risk Analysis and Risk Management (includes the key scripture—Remember—to memorize during that week's study). If you read the assigned chapters in *Risk,* which I strongly recommend, plan on investing at least two hours on each lesson.

2. *One-on-one study* for you and an accountability partner. This may be the best way to get the most benefit from this workbook. Each week, both you and your partner will do your individual study of the session material. Then you will get together to discuss the content and work as a team on some one-on-one questions and exercises (Risk Assessment—Man to Man).

3. *Small group discussion guide.* Men appreciate getting together to hear each other's opinions, share some laughs, study the Word, encourage one another, and pray. Each session of the *Risk Workbook* includes a list of questions (Risk and Reward—Small Group Discussion) intended for such a gathering of men. These discussions will be most rewarding if every participant completes the personal workbook study before the small group meeting.

The end of each session includes the suggested readings and assignment for the next week.

No matter how you use the *Risk Workbook,* you will have abundant opportunities to go deeper in your faith and realize the rewards of a risk-oriented walk with God. However, you will experience the maximum results if you participate in every element: personal workbook, one-on-one study, and small group discussion.

The workbook includes ample space for you to write your answers, comments, and questions. A special page—the Risk Journal—follows the conclusion of each session. This is a place for you to write any ideas, conclusions, challenges, and personal insights that you found meaningful in that week's session.

The *Risk Workbook* is designed for an eight-week time frame. However, if it takes you longer to complete the study personally—or as a small group—take all the time you need. It is not unusual for a group to spend two or three meetings completing one lesson. Always go for depth over distance—every time.

Before you begin each study, commit your time to God. Ask the Holy Spirit to illumine your mind, guide your heart, and energize your spirit as you read each section and answer each question.

Above all, please adapt this workbook so that it truly works for *you.* This is your workbook, your invitation to know God better, your opportunity to explore what a more passionate devotion to God means—your life of *risk.*

introduction

Before we begin, I thought you might find interesting what some others have said about risk and related subjects:

> The greatest risk is the risk of riskless living.
>
> —Stephen Covey

> The pessimist sees the difficulty in every opportunity; an optimist sees the opportunity in every difficulty.
>
> —Winston Churchill

> You've got to go out on a limb sometimes because that's where the fruit is.
>
> —Will Rogers

> One doesn't discover new lands without consenting to lose sight of the shore for a very long time.
>
> —André Gide

> You've got to jump off cliffs all the time and build your wings on the way down.
>
> —Ray Bradbury

> The important thing is this: To be able at any moment to sacrifice what we are for what we could become.
>
> —Charles Du Bos

There is no security on this earth, there is only opportunity.

—Douglas MacArthur

Bite off more than you can chew, then chew it.

—Anonymous

Creativity requires the courage to let go of certainties.

—Erich Fromm

A life spent making mistakes is not only more honorable, but more useful than a life spent doing nothing.

—George Bernard Shaw

Life is either a daring adventure or nothing. Security does not exist in nature, nor do the children of men as a whole experience it. Avoiding danger is no safer in the long run than exposure.

—Helen Keller

A rut is nothing but a grave—with both ends kicked out.

—Vance Havner

I am not afraid of storms, for I am learning how to sail my ship.

—Louisa May Alcott

Twenty years from now you will be more disappointed by the things that you didn't do than by the ones you did do. So throw off the bowlines. Sail away from the safe harbor. Catch the trade winds in your sails. Explore. Dream. Discover.

—Mark Twain

> I am always doing that which I cannot do, in order that I may learn how to do it.
>
> —Pablo Picasso

> In skating over thin ice, our safety is in our speed.
>
> —Ralph Waldo Emerson

> 'Tis better to have loved and lost, than never to have loved at all.
>
> —Alfred, Lord Tennyson

> Restlessness and discontent are the first necessities of progress.
>
> —Thomas A. Edison

> It doesn't work to leap a twenty-foot chasm in two ten-foot jumps.
>
> —American Proverb

Well, that's a hearty meal of food for thought!

It's obvious that the topic of risk stirs the mind and senses. Throughout history, people have longed to test the limits, to push the boundaries of personal courage, to face the unknown, to lock the door and leave the comfort zone, to leap and trust God for a safe landing.

The early church knew many big risk takers. You will recall "Barnabas and Paul—men who…risked their lives for the name of our Lord Jesus Christ" (Acts 15:25–26).

Then there was a fellow, not as well known, perhaps, named Epaphroditus. This is what the apostle Paul said about him: "Welcome him with Christian love and with great joy, and be sure to honor people like him. For he risked his life for the work of Christ" (Philippians 2:29–30, NLT).

I want to be known as a risk taker for God. The heartbeat quickens when we face our fears and take action for a great and noble cause. We were made for such a life, to follow in the footsteps of the supreme risk taker of all, the One who defines sacrifice and glorious guts—Jesus Christ.

Here's something He said about His own riskiness: "I am the Good Shepherd. The Good Shepherd risks and lays down His [own] life for the sheep" (John 10:11, AMP).

Jesus once said to His first disciples, who had freaked out when He went walking on the water: "Take courage! It is I. Don't be afraid." (Matthew 14:27).

That's how we will do this—become God's men ready to risk it all for the only cause that really matters.

Are you ready for some risk?

Me too.

1

risk taking

This week's session is based on chapter 1, "Inner Turbulence," and chapter 2, "Mach 1 Loyalty," in Risk.

I think that every man, at heart, wants to be a risk taker. And as we will learn together through study of this workbook, the greatest risk opportunity of all is to be a sold-out follower of Jesus Christ.

> 📖 Risk is in the DNA of every man, put there by God and for God. You may have misplaced it, neglected it, misused it, but it is time to get it back. It is time to do something great for God with it *right now.* 📖

Just how do we do that? How do we get from where we are in our walk with Christ to where we want to be? Let's find out together. But before we begin…

Throughout this workbook you will find excerpts from my book *Risk.* These will be identified by this icon: 📖. I highly recommend that you read the companion chapters from the book. (I know, I wrote it. But really, there is a lot of dynamite material in the book that I won't repeat here.) I've also included special sections in this workbook to set up the questions I want you to answer as we discover what it means to be a world-class risk taker on behalf of our Lord and the kingdom of God.

Risk Analysis

Predictability. Control. Safety. Comfort. The book *Risk* explores God's views on those subjects and how they fit or, more precisely, don't fit into your quest to become God's man.

I hate to say it, but I think too many Christian men are missing out on the only adventure that really counts in life—walking with God and carrying out His plans for the advancement of His cause here on the earth. We are supposed to be like Jesus, right? Would you describe him as a guy who played it safe?

> 📖 Like all God's men, the first disciples had their own "Oh, mama" moments with Christ. Each was on a journey to fulfill God's purposes for his life. Aware of this, Jesus knew he had to address the whole issue of risky commitment if the disciples were to succeed in their mission after He'd conquered the Cross. He was direct and uncomfortably honest. 📖

> From the days of John the Baptist until now, the kingdom of heaven has been forcefully advancing, and *forceful men* lay hold of it. (Matthew 11:12, emphasis added)

> If anyone would come after me, he must deny himself and take up his cross and follow me. (Matthew 16:24)

> If anyone comes to me and does not hate his father and mother, his wife and children, his brothers and sisters—yes, even his own life—he cannot be my disciple. (Luke 14:26)

1. What do you think playing it safe means in the context of a man's life?

2. Why do you think so many Christian men seem to play it safe in their relationship with God?

Boys Will Be Boys

Nobody had to teach me how to take risks when I was a boy. I just naturally seemed eager to "push the edge" as I went about my play. I particularly found my big-goose-bump thrills while jumping:

> Tension. Unpredictability. Letting go. Adrenaline.
>
> Oh yeah, baby. Jumping off of things is in our DNA. It took me about two seconds to come up with my short list of things I used to love jumping off.

> The roof into a cold pool. Trampolines. The swings. A pogo stick to Billy Joel music, eight hundred and fifty seven times in my parents' garage. Over Calabasas Creek with my yellow Schwinn. Into mischief for the simple thrill of it. . . . Our fathers (or mothers) looked at us and said, "What were you thinking?" We said, "I don't know." And that was the truth: there *was* no explanation! We were boys. We were stretching the limits of our courage, testing the limits of our abilities, risking injury for the rush of what was on the other side of the experience. We lived for that freedom and risked life and limb naturally.

1. What are some things you remember doing as a boy that were a little risky?

2. Was there a point in your growing up when you started taking fewer risks? Why did that happen?

It's not just general risk taking that seems to diminish as a boy grows and becomes a man. There can be a decline in jumping spiritually too. After starting strong with Christ, too many men lose their spiritual passion and often get distracted by other loyalties and priorities.

As I work with men all over the world, they tell me about their battles to break through the inner spiritual barrier of total loyalty to Jesus Christ. Whether it's soldiers e-mailing me from Iraq or guys in my own congregation, they all lament disloyalty to their King and are frustrated by their lapses in spiritual loyalty. It eats at them that they cannot seem to break through and enter that new realm of spiritual life and loyalty that noble men of God possess in abundance....

The gaps in their lives lead many men to make the fatal mistake of lowering the bar of God's Word so as not to be on the hook for strong passages like "Just as he who called you is holy, so be holy in all you do" (1 Peter 1:15). In our shame, we desensitize our spirits to His voice, become critical of others who are succeeding, and, in the process, achieve new spiritual lows....

All God's men are called to break through the spiritual loyalty barrier and move from a fragile and fickle heart commitment to a fierce loyalty in Christ.

3. Why do you think God set such high standards for His children, for example, asking us to "be holy in all [we] do"?

4. Are there areas in your life where you struggle to stay loyal to the standards Christ has set? If so, make a list of your areas of struggle. Remember, this is your workbook and this is not a test. Be brutally honest with yourself.

Spiritual Turbulence

I believe that our loyalties drive our priorities, and those priorities drive our choices. And those choices determine how committed we become in our relationships with God and others.

1. At this point in your life, what would you say are your top five priorities for yourself?

2. Look at the list you just made. How does each of these priorities enhance or detract from your loyalty to Jesus Christ?

In *Risk* I tell the story of Chuck Yeager, the famous test pilot who was the first man to crack the sound barrier by achieving supersonic speed. As his plane increased its air speed to a subsonic level just before the breaking of the sound barrier, the aircraft experienced significant turbulence. I believe something similar happens to us spiritually as we increase our loyalty to Christ and take action more aggressively on His behalf.

📖 In our quest to experience the power and freedom total loyalty to Jesus provides God's man, we are bound to encounter problems, obstacles, challenges, and doubts about ever being free of our sinful and dark desires. Chuck Yeager's journey is a lot like our own, peppered with passion for God mixed with doubts about ourselves, turbulent spiritual forces, and unforeseen obstacles.

3. Can you recall any experiences when you felt unusual challenges or opposition as you sought to increase your level of loyalty to Jesus? List several examples.

4. Right now, as you consider how to be more sold out for God, what do you think are your toughest obstacles?

Taking Risks for God

In *Risk* I identify four principles that I think any man who wants to follow God with all his heart needs to embrace. So that each principle is easier to remember, I start each idea with a word that begins with a letter from the word RISK.

Right view of God
Identity settled
Sacrifice like Christ
Kingdom-build

Let's briefly review each principle, then we'll unpack the meaning so that you can make sure each of these principles is alive and well in your life.

Right View of God

Our down-in-our-gut view of God determines so much of what we think, how we act, and who we really are. Is God sovereign or not? Does God know everything or not? Is He present everywhere at all times or not? Is it possible to have a personal relationship with God or not? Is God good and kind or not? Our answers to these questions are important. A. W. Tozer wrote: "Were we to extract from any man a complete answer to the question, 'What comes into your mind when you think about God?' we might predict with certainty the spiritual future of that man."

Jesus knew God and knew precisely what he thought of God. That's why it says in the New Testament:

> They came to him and said, "Teacher, we know you are a man of integrity. *You aren't swayed by men, because you pay no attention to who they are;* but you teach the way of God in accordance with the truth." (Mark 12:14, emphasis added)

1. Here's a great exercise to define your personal viewpoint: In one hundred words or less, write out your personal statement of who God is.

2. What parts of your personal definition of God could use elaboration or more study?

Identity Settled

"But you, *man of God,* flee from all this, and pursue righteousness, godliness, faith, love, endurance and gentleness. *Fight* the good fight of the faith. *Take hold* of the eternal life to which you were called when you made your good confession in the presence of many witnesses" (1 Timothy 6:11–12, emphasis added).

Paul knew that the quickest and most effective way to pull greatness out of his pupil Timothy was to remind him of who he *really* was. He might be tempted to pretend to be someone else, but Timothy was God's man—that was his identity. His mentor knew that his identity shaped his loyalty and that loyalty is what drives our choices. In Timothy's life it meant fleeing inconsistent identities, fighting hard for what he believed, and being loyal to his calling as God's man.

3. Most men, when they meet a man they don't know, will not wait too long to ask, "Well, what do you do?" Why do you think men are so interested in knowing what someone else does?

4. How much of your impression of your identity, value, and importance is based on what you do in your job or career?

5. In what areas (personal, family, career, social, church) of your life do you feel you are firmly established or identified as God's man?

6. In what areas do you need to become better identified as God's man?

Sacrifice Like Christ

If we walk obediently with Christ, inevitably we will find ourselves sacrificing and suffering for His way of living and His cause. This is a good thing, though, not some hardship that should cause us to grit our teeth and whine, "Why me?" Check out this verse:

> In bringing many sons to glory, it was fitting that God, for whom and through whom everything exists, should make the author of their salvation perfect through suffering. Both the one who makes men holy and *those who are made holy* are of the same family. So Jesus is not ashamed to call them brothers. (Hebrews 2:10–11, emphasis added)

Since God lives in you and calls you a son, He will make you perfect, too, by calling you to self-sacrifice. *Really*—what a great honor! A benefit of this is that sacrifice *for* Christ is what unites us most deeply *with* Christ. That's why the apostle Paul wrote, "I want to know Christ and the power of his resurrection and *the fellowship of sharing in his sufferings*" (Philippians 3:10, emphasis added).

> 🕮 Few of us will be called to give our lives, millions of us will be called to sacrifice our wills for His will, material wealth for spiritual wealth, earthly recognition for heavenly recognition, carnal appetites for godly appetites, career dreams for God's dream, corporate ladders for family health, and convenient compromise for spiritual integrity. Sacrifice and suffering loss for the sake of our faith is what connects the God-Man and God's man....
>
> Risking for God is synonymous with sacrificing for God, and it is not a burden; it is a privilege as God's man. It is a special bond we share with Christ and part of our worship. We lay our lives on the altar so He can use us mightily for His work. 🕮

7. In our culture today, why does the idea of self-sacrifice seem like such a difficult—even negative—experience?

8. Recall a time or two when you were very aware that you were making a sacrifice for Jesus. What were these experiences like? How did you feel about your relationship with Christ during these times?

Kingdom-Build

Our final RISK principle puts it all together as we work to advance the kingdom of God.

> It's time to invest in something you can't take with you but something you can send ahead to eternity. It's time to get busy building the kingdom of God right where you live, in your local church, and in your world. It's time to start thinking outside the box and dream—dream big God dreams.
>
> The kingdom doesn't need more religious guys. It requires more big, hairy, audacious dreamers.

> The kingdom mentality is not for the spiritually timid; it is for the man of war. And it *is* about winning—souls, communities, people in desperation, countries in darkness, and all the particular battles of your world. It's about winning men you know to join forces and affect the course of history.

9. How would you answer the question, What is the kingdom of God?

10. Why is a kingdom mentality not for the spiritually timid?

11. How do you believe God has called you to take risks in being a kingdom builder?

I cannot think of any rush or high more exhilarating, demanding, and ultimately fulfilling than laying it all on the line for Jesus! Won't you join me in living a life of RISK?

Risk Management

Each session, as you complete the Risk Analysis section of the *Risk Workbook,* I will ask you to spend a few minutes summarizing what we have covered. An important part of living a sold-out life for Christ is to grasp the meaning of the Word of God and capitalize on its power—just like Jesus did throughout His life on earth. I urge you to memorize a crucial verse in each session, which will always be highlighted under the Remember heading.

Remember

> [Jesus] called his disciples and the crowds to come over and listen. "If any of you wants to be my follower," he told them, "you must put aside your selfish ambition, shoulder your cross, and follow me. If you try to keep your life for yourself, you will lose it. But if you give up your life for my sake and for the sake of the Good News, you will find true life." (Mark 8:34–35, NLT)

Reflect

1. In this session's Remember scripture, Jesus says that if we want to follow him, we need to do three things. They are:

   __________ your selfish ambition
   __________ your cross
   __________ me

2. How would you rate yourself in each of these three areas on a 1 to 10 scale: 1 meaning "I'm failing horribly" to 10 meaning "I'm world class at this."

   ___ putting aside selfish ambition
   ___ shouldering your cross
   ___ following Jesus

3. How might you improve your rating on each of Jesus's requirements for being His disciple?

Respond

In the next week, find one thing to do for someone else that will cause you to sacrifice something and advance the kingdom of God. Write here what you plan to do and how you will do it.

In chapter 10 of *Risk,* I describe what aggressive accountability looks like. Since I want you to start now to get involved in a healthy accountability relationship with at least one other man, here I will describe (based on material in the book) the elements of such a relationship.

Space Invasion

What does aggressive accountability (what I describe as space invasion) look like? When I have been placed by God in community with another man for the purposes of spiritual growth and have his permission and willingness to be accountable, I need to emphasize the same things Paul did with *every man:* "We *proclaim* Him, *admonishing* every man and *teaching* every man with all wisdom, so that we may *present* every man *complete* in Christ. For this purpose also I labor, striving according to His power, which mightily works within me" (Colossians 1:28–29, NASB, emphasis added).

Let's look at each of these elements in order:

Proclamation. Space invasion is an outreach to another man. It is evangelistic in the sense that we are reaching out to another brother in Jesus's name and for His sake, not our own. More simply, Christ is front and center in the accountability relationship. The filter through which advice is given, problems are resolved, and issues are settled is Jesus Christ. Above all, the relationship expresses a commitment to Him and His will. "Whatever you do, whether in word or deed, do it all in the name of the Lord Jesus, giving thanks to God the Father through him" (Colossians 3:17).

Admonition. Space invasion is filled with gentle and firm warnings against evil. Notice I didn't say slow warnings. When there is a moral, sexual, relational, financial, or spiritual temptation, we come out strongly based on God's Word. We don't have to be loud; God's Word will do the piercing and the cutting to the heart of a man. We are on patrol and watching the bushes for enemy movement from within and without. We do spiritual warfare together.

Education. Space invasion is all about learning spiritually from another man or "teaching every man in all wisdom." Each person has his unique strengths and weaknesses, and we mutually offer and receive those in order to be stronger God's men. Jesus stated very clearly that God's man is to be about the business of "teaching them to observe all that I commanded you"

(Matthew 28:20, NASB) for as long as we have got a pulse. What we receive from God spiritually (insight, wisdom, spiritual gifts) we are to give away to other men.

Presentation. Space invasion is all about pushing a man to *live out* his values. In a sense, Paul says that he puts his spiritual investments (other men) on display for people to see. He says that proclamation, admonition, and education are for a distinct purpose: "so that we may present every man." The guys close to him are proudly displayed men of character. Each reflects the time, effort, and personal training he has invested. That's why space invaders—godly guys who love the Lord and you so much that they just won't pull punches—are so important. They're the men who push hard on the issue of spiritual integrity and being undivided about what we say and what we do. When you're a space invader, your men are walking billboards of your efforts. You will not let them fail on your watch if you can help it.

Completion. Space invasion is about canvassing *every domain* of a man's relationship with God and with people. The end game is full maturity—completeness in Christ. We want our accountability partner to be mature, lacking nothing in his moral, marital, spiritual, and family life. We seek the full development of God's purposes by watching his connection to other men (fellowship). We ask about his time spent with Jesus through prayer, confession, and Scripture intake (discipleship). We discern his heart for and love for Jesus (worship). We encourage him to continue to develop and use his spiritual gifts to minister to other believers (service). We make sure he is seeking out opportunities to tell someone else what Christ has done in his life (evangelism).

 Risk Assessment (Man to Man)

As you already know, if you've read much of *Risk* or heard me speak (or just read the sidebar), I believe strongly that becoming a fully effective God's man requires you to have an honest, strong accountability relationship with at least one godly man. In each session I will list several questions for you to ask each other—ideally at a time when you get together each week to find out how life is going, to feast on the Word, and to pray.

Take turns asking each other these questions:

1. How do you see yourself—are you a person who takes a lot of risks, or are you more cautious?
2. In what part of your Christian life do you think you should take more risks?
3. Share personal needs and requests, and pray for each other.

 Risk and Reward (Small Group Discussion)

1. Do you agree that "risk is in the DNA of every man"? What are the reasons for your answer?
2. Here are four actions that involve high risk: skydiving, whitewater kayaking, rock climbing, deep-sea diving. Which of these makes your stomach the most weak? Why?
3. Why do you think Jesus selected "selfish ambition" as the first issue that His followers had to get rid of?
4. When Jesus said that any follower of His had to "shoulder [his] cross," what thoughts would run through the mind of a man living in the first century? (Clue: Have you seen the movie *The Passion of the Christ*?)

5. In our world today, what are some examples of what it might mean for a God's man to lose his life?
6. What do you think Jesus meant by the term "true life"?

 Risk Behavior

Here's what needs to happen before the next small group meeting:

1. Complete your personal study of session 2, which includes reading chapters 3, 4, and 5 in *Risk.*
2. Meet with your accountability partner.
3. Accomplish the Risk task you listed under Respond in the Risk Management section on page 21.
4. Record any of your observations in the Risk Journal.

Risk Journal

____

____

____

____

____

2

"be it so"

This week's session is based on chapter 3, "One Man's Obedience," chapter 4, "Liked or Faithful?" and chapter 5, "You Are the Solution," in Risk.

The world has known some great risk takers for the gospel. The most risky one of all, of course, was the Lord Jesus, who risked everything so that humanity (that would be you and I) could have life. The disciples followed Jesus's lead: All of them experienced a violent death, except for the apostle John who died in exile on the Isle of Patmos. I can't believe any of these men wanted a martyr's death, but their courageous willingness to shed their blood was the stimulus for the explosive, worldwide spread of the good news, and it laid the foundation of the church.

We launch this week's study with a brief look at a saint and hero of the early church named Ignatius. His stirring, give-it-all-up devotion makes my attempts to stand strong for Christ look kind of wimpy. But with all my heart I want to become a "Be it so" kind of man. I think you will too.

Risk Analysis

Push came to shove for Ignatius too. As the head pastor of the church in Antioch, he was recalled to Rome by Emperor Trajan because he unashamedly taught and professed Christ in Syria. While in Smyrna, he sent a communication ahead to the Roman Christians asking them to do something very unusual—don't intervene!

"Now I begin to be a disciple. I care for nothing of visible or invisible things so that I may but win Christ. Let fire and the cross, let the companies of wild beasts, let the breaking of the bones and the tearing of limbs, let the grinding of the whole body, and all the malice of the devil come upon me; be it so, only may I win Christ Jesus."

On the day of his execution, with the sounds of the roaring lions as the backdrop, his desire to suffer with Christ moved him to say, "I am the wheat of Christ; I am going to be ground with the teeth of wild beasts that I may be found pure bread."[1]...

"Be it so" are the words of a man who has stopped caring about what men think—especially powerful men like the emperor Trajan. If Ignatius were living among us in the digital age, he would never, like many men today, tremble at the thought of disappointing people, bosses, friends, peers, neighbors, or the guy in seat 22A next to him. Instead of being incapable of direct and strong speech about his Savior, he would tell his story and leave the results in God's hands....

"Be it so" are the words of a God's man whose personal commitments, actions, and words have zilch to do with living up to the expectations or standards of other people. Being faithful to Christ replaces being liked by people.

1. John Foxe, *The New Foxe's Book of Martyrs* (North Brunswick, NJ: Bridge-Logos, 1997), 14.

1. What do you think Ignatius meant when he said, "Be it so, only *may I win Christ Jesus*"?

2. Are you aware of or do you know personally anyone alive today who displays this kind of stunning courage for the gospel? What impresses you most about this person?

So do not throw away your confidence; it will be richly rewarded. You need to persevere so that when you have done the will of God, you will receive what he has promised. For in just a very little while,

"He who is coming will come and will not delay.
    But my righteous one will live by faith.
And if he shrinks back,
    I will not be pleased with him."

But we are not of those who shrink back and are destroyed, but of those who believe and are saved. (Hebrews 10:35–39)

📖 Loss of a strong identity in Christ has created a culture of Christian men who are more at ease chasing cool and being liked. We want to be admired and respected but not really known. Sexual conquest, physical attractiveness, recognition, and status have landed many of God's men in a stupor of self-importance and spiritual insignificance.

3. What might be some examples of shrinking-back behavior for a man living in today's world?

4. In your own experience, what are some situations when you find it difficult to take a strong stand for Christ and the gospel?

The Cost of Discipleship

Prior to World War II, the famous German pastor and theologian Dietrich Bonhoeffer wrote a book entitled *The Cost of Discipleship.* In the book he said, "When Christ calls a man, he bids him come and die." Bonhoeffer lived out the truth in his words. Because he resisted Hitler's regime, he was imprisoned and executed by hanging in 1945, just months before the war ended.[2]

---

2. Dietrich Bonhoeffer, *The Cost of Discipleship* (New York: Touchstone, 1995), 89.

Following Jesus is meant to cost us something—it can range from feeling some embarrassment when the guys at work laugh because they found out you've been to a church men's retreat, to the ultimate sacrifice of martyrdom.

> Following Jesus Christ inevitably means coming to a crossroads about whom you will live to please. Our King did not take great pains to, shall we say, put His guys at ease before sending them out to represent Him. But He was honest about the cost and what He expected from them. There would be no 401(k), no health benefits, no salary, no company donkeys. Just repeated attempts at intimidation.
>
> Would you have signed up for this?
>
> "A student is not greater than the teacher. A servant is not greater than the master. The student shares the teacher's fate. The servant shares the master's fate....
>
> "Don't be afraid of those who want to kill you. They can only kill your body; they cannot touch your soul. Fear only God, who can destroy both soul and body in hell....
>
> "If anyone acknowledges me publicly here on earth, I will openly acknowledge that person before my Father in heaven. But if anyone denies me here on earth, I will deny that person before my Father in heaven" (Matthew 10:24–25, 28, 32–33, NLT).

1. What do you think Jesus meant when He said, "A student is not greater than the teacher.... The student shares the master's fate"?

2. In today's world, what would be an example or two of how someone might deny Jesus "here on the earth"?

📖 A commander briefing his troops before a combat mission doesn't say to his platoon, "Okay, men. This is gonna be a cakewalk. When we get up there, the enemy is going to be so amazed by us, they'll throw down their guns and ask how they can be like us.... On the contrary, Jesus says, "Men, they're gonna come at you with both barrels blazing. But we'll stand our ground. Don't you be intimidated. You've got a bigger gun. I'm your leader here." 📖

3. Although the potential cost of following Christ is high, what are some of God's promises from Scripture that give us courage and strength as we enter into battle with Him?

Saying Yes to God

What we do—even the most inconsequential actions—matters. This was true at the very beginning.

Just as the result of one trespass was condemnation for all men, so also the result of one act of righteousness was justification that brings life for all men. For just as through the disobedience of the one man the many were made sinners, so also through the obedience of the one man the many will be made righteous. (Romans 5:18–19)

📖 One man's obedience brings life to many. We simply do not know how far-reaching one act of obedience to God will be and what consequences our choice will have for others. This reason alone would be enough to seek God's will in all matters. When the moment of our greatest challenge arrives, we want to be in the habit of saying yes to God rather than debating or compromising. Being ready means we aren't considering our own rewards or consequences, but the impact of our choices upon others....

Spiritual obedience and spiritual disobedience set in motion consequences we cannot undo. 📖

1. In your experience, can you recall an event when a choice you or someone else made had a dramatic impact on others?

2. What do you find most difficult about being obedient—that is, doing what you know God wants you to do?

The Obedience and Gratitude Link

> 🕮 The guys at Saddleback Church are used to hearing me say, "If you don't have an attitude of gratitude, all you have left is *attitude*." 🕮

Have you had a mean boss? A taskmaster coach? Maybe even an overly strict or abusive father? It's hard to obey someone in authority who is unreasonable or a jerk. But when we are asked to obey God, we are submitting to Someone who loves us dearly and has only our best interests in mind. I have to tell you—I love giving back to God; He is so incredibly cool and has done so much for me!

> 🕮 It doesn't matter if you're a pastor of a thirty-thousand-member church or a brand-new believer. The questions for God's men are always: *Am I going to do life my way or God's way? What does God require of me in this situation? What is God telling me? What does His Word say? What will honor Him most? Am I going to trust God's promise or try to make it happen on my own?*
>
> Obedience is the evidence that convinces the world that we are indeed grateful. What's pathetic is a man who has been the recipient of this grace and mercy but doesn't act like one. 🕮

> We know that we have come to know [the Lord] if we obey his commands. The man who says, "I know him," but does not do what he commands is a liar, and the truth is not in him. But if anyone obeys his word, God's love is truly made complete in him. (1 John 2:3–5)

1. Think back through your life: Is there someone you hated to obey? What about the opposite—someone you would do anything for? What caused the difference in your response?

2. Why do you think our obedience is so important to God?

3. What are the areas in your life where you find it most difficult to trust God?

It makes all the sense in the world that Jesus would not call us to faith and make obedience a burden. In fact, He chastised the toxic legalism of the Pharisees severely. Then He promised us He would show us love and commitment, and we, as His brothers, would respond with commitment of our own. "Greater love has no one than this, that he lay down his life for his friends. You are my friends if you do what I command" (John 15:13–14)....

"I have considered my ways and have turned my steps to your statutes. I will hasten and not delay to obey your commands" (Psalm 119:59–60). 📖

4. Jesus said that if we obey His commands, we are His friends. How might friendship with Jesus make obeying Him easier for you?

Show Me the Obedience

Ultimately, if we are to become "Be it so" God's men, our actions must be the proof of our obedience. You remember that crude playground challenge, "Put up or shut up"? Will we be the man who is known for doing the right thing instead of only thinking or talking about it?

We know that God honors our raw commitment to follow Him and do what He says. We don't have to be superstar saints. We need to grateful grunts. And when we give Him who we are and what we have, look out!

📖 Great thoughts—the ones that are selfless—are from God.... Nurtured with faith, those great thoughts for God, combined with faithful actions, produced great results that brought great glory to God. It's *so* like Jesus to take our little and make more.

"When Jesus looked up and saw a great crowd coming toward him, he said to Philip, 'Where shall we buy bread for these people to eat?' He asked this only to test him, for he already had in mind what he was going to do.

"Philip answered him, 'Eight months' wages would not buy enough bread for each one to have a bite!'

"Another of his disciples, Andrew, Simon Peter's brother, spoke up. 'Here is a boy with five small barley loaves and two small fish, but how far will they go among so many?'

"Jesus said, 'Have the people sit down' " (John 6:5–10).

Philip gives Jesus a mouthful. The boy gives Jesus a sack full. Andrew remains doubtful. Way to go, boys; no gold stars for you today. *That* one goes to the seven-year-old who saw and heard a need, came to Jesus, and gave what he had. Tell a little kid you can't afford to sponsor a Compassion child and she comes back holding up her piggy bank. Children don't know what it costs and they don't care. They're just focused on a solution. 📖

1. Why do you think the little boy "got" Jesus while His disciples didn't get it?

2. What among your talents or resources might be the "little" loaves and fishes that God could turn into something great for the benefit of His kingdom?

3. Here's a set of prompts that might help you answer the previous question. Trust God to speak to you through your answers to these questions:

- What are the things you care about the most *as a man?*

- What's your natural skill set?

- Where do you get results versus failure?

- What subjects do you love to talk about?

- Where do you like to invest your physical energy?

- In what situations do you find yourself getting most competitive?

- What are core parts of your testimony as a Christian?

- What did you struggle with as a nonbeliever?

- What do you continue to struggle with?

- Where are you most energized spiritually?

- What has been the biggest loss you've ever suffered?

- When did you feel the most pain?

- If you could do anything for God, what would it be?

📖 God will not call you to a specific ministry without having you consider the honest answers to these questions. He wants to use *everything* that you are—not just the pretty pieces but also the painful parts that you don't like to bring up.

Authentic manhood versus synthetic manhood is a matter of honesty. When you are honest with God, self, and others, you are a free man: free to serve with all that you are versus wearing masks to hide insecurities....

As you begin to take more risks and become a solution to the needs around you in the name of your King, God will progressively increase both the scope and the scale of the risks you need to take for Him. Risk for a toddler is jumping into Daddy's arms in the pool. Risk for my ten-year-old is dropping in a quarter pipe at the skate park. Risk for a high-school senior is standing up for what's unpopular. And so on. God will always call you to progressively aggressive faith in step with your growth. He knows just how to stretch us.

Risk Management

Remember

Whoever has my commands and obeys them, he is the one who loves me. He who loves me will be loved by my Father, and I too will love him and show myself to him. (John 14:21)

Reflect

1. Why do you think Jesus ties the evidence of real love for Him so tightly to obeying Him?

2. What do you think Jesus meant when He said that He would "show myself to him"? How does Jesus "show" or reveal Himself to you?

Respond

This week, select one area of your life where you want to improve your obedience to Christ. Write it down here, and also state what the proof of this obedience will be.

 Risk Assessment (Man to Man)

Report to each other any memorable events in your spiritual journey from the previous week. Be sure to mention answers to prayer and praise reports.

1. The book *Risk* contains a list of things that in obedience we might have to risk giving up for God—perhaps at great personal cost. Discuss these items together. Has either of you ever had to sacrifice anything like this for the kingdom? What was the result?
   - losing money
   - losing a relationship
   - losing a good feeling
   - losing a secret
   - losing a job opportunity
   - losing your image at church
   - losing friends
   - losing possessions
   - losing a dream
   - losing the privilege of doing things *your* way
2. Share with each other at least one thing God has taught you recently. Wrap up with prayer.

Risk and Reward (Small Group Discussion)

1. For a few minutes, take turns sharing any "Be it so" examples you are aware of—situations when you or someone you know stood up bravely for Christ or the gospel.
2. Why do you think so many Christian men today seem so concerned with "chasing cool" or being liked?
3. The book *Risk* says, "God's men have to kiss the middle ground good-bye." What do you think is meant by that?
4. Hebrews 12:1 says, "Since we are surrounded by such a great cloud of witnesses, let us throw off everything that hinders and the sin that so easily entangles, and

let us run with perseverance the race marked out for us." When it comes to obedience to God, what issues seem to hinder you most? What sins entangle the worst?

5. What joys and blessings await the man who faithfully obeys God? What are the rewards in this life? What are the rewards in heaven?

Now that you know these things, you will be blessed if you do them.
(John 13:17)

Risk Behavior

Here's what needs to happen before the next small group meeting:

1. Complete your personal study of session 3, which includes reading chapters 6, 7, and 8 in *Risk.*
2. Meet with your accountability partner.
3. Accomplish the Risk task you listed under Respond in the Risk Management section on page 40.
4. Record any of your observations in the Risk Journal.

Risk Journal

____

____

____

3

created for worship

This week's session is based on chapter 6, "Ruthless Pursuit," chapter 7, "Passionate Sons," and chapter 8, "Same Is Not the Enemy," in Risk.

I fulfilled a lifelong dream in 2005 while on a trip to London by touring the British Museum—arguably the greatest museum in the world. I was not disappointed with my hours there, which could have been days. For over 250 years the world has deposited many of its great treasures at this museum.

I enjoyed the collections, but I won't bore you with a room-by-room review. I did see one little sign, though, that relates to a theme of this lesson: the sign was titled "Secular Life in the Middle Ages." Underneath was a line that read "Trade, feasting, and warfare dominated secular life in the Middle Ages."

Hmm. I guess life hasn't changed much in the last thousand years or so. What men often are passionate for now—stuff, good times, power—that's what was occupying the guys back in the Middle Ages!

As God's men we need to get it. Life does not revolve around our natural appetites. There's something bigger and more important than a thick steak, a warm babe, and a two-seat convertible. We have the incredible option of turning away from those things and fixing our gaze on Almighty God. That should stir our red, manly blood.

So where's the passion?

Risk Analysis

> 🕮 God's man is called to invest his passions in the service of life, not invest his life in the service of his passions. God knows that we have energy to devote to something, and He designed that energy to be put toward knowing and loving Him—in worship....
>
> Sadly, millions of Christian men...start off in awe and "magic" as salvation invades our soul. But slowly our spiritual high is tempered by some of the realities of spiritual growth that are going to have to be worked out rather than "magically" resolved.... We are disillusioned. Slowly but surely our walk with God becomes familiar and routine. The raging fire has dwindled to a tiny ember that doesn't provide light or comfort to those around it. We are simply going though the motions and begin to look toward other outlets to be passionate about. 🕮

1. Why do you think spiritual passion seems to diminish over time in the lives of so many followers of Christ?

2. If you have ever felt as if you were just "going through the motions" in your Christian life, why do you think that happened?

Many of us have stories of God's supernatural intervention and reassurance in times of fear.... Having fought and won some major battles for the kingdom, we God's men commonly become overconfident in our successes. At these times, the challenge is continuing to work *through* the stages of our spiritual journeys, allowing God to direct us to our next missions.

The fact is that growth, spiritual expansion, victory, and exciting new experiences in Christ await. And they will create a whole new level of spiritual battle. This new foe will not be looking so much to exploit your failure as to get you resting on your success. Few men are prepared for this new character test. Ironically, spiritual success is the *ultimate* test, since the Enemy never simply lies down and gives up just because you've got a good spiritual routine going.

3. Have you ever had a spiritual high followed by a frustrating spiritual low? What happened? Have you discovered ways to avoid this experience?

4. In what areas of your life are you most aware of the enemy's attacks and spiritual warfare against you?

📖 Remember, you will never "arrive" until you arrive. As in, "Hello, Jesus, nice place you got here" arrive. The Bible is clear that down here we'll never arrive. We simply keep fighting, becoming more like Christ with every "success," remembering that the only true success is the one that points to Him. "Just as you received Christ Jesus as Lord, continue to live in him, rooted and built up in him, strengthened in the faith as you were taught, and overflowing with thankfulness" (Colossians 2:6–7). 📖

5. What are some ways you have found to keep your commitment to Christ steady and passionate?

Watch What You Worship

I have found that one of the best ways to fight complacency and stagnation in my journey with Christ is to keep my worship current and robust. We were created for worship, so it's good to make sure we are giving our devotion and adoration to God, not to the many idols that surround us and constantly entice our affection.

Polluting your worship of Christ is Satan's goal, and he will try to infect it by introducing worldly desires to increase, indulge, and impress. He wants to put sand in the gas tank of your spiritual life and tube your relationships with God and people. He will work hard to get you to blend worldly passions into the fabric of your godliest passions....

[Satan] likes hoodwinking God's men because he knows that pursuers of power, enthusiastic indulgers, and men passionate about possessions share one common denominator: a low view of people and a broken relationship with God.

1. What does worship of God mean to you? Write your personal definition here.

2. What things, activities, attitudes, and relationships in your life seem most likely to pollute and diminish your passionate worship of God?

Don't worship things or begin to be more concerned about money and things you own (or don't) than about God and people. Ask: *Am I in bondage to credit-card bills? Am I tithing regularly? Am I being generous? Am I trying to impress others by what I drive or wear? Am I being a good steward of God's money? Am I obsessing over a toy?...*

Ask: *Am I searching for stuff on TV? Am I addicted to sexual Happy Meals? Am I loving my wife? Am I enslaved by lustful thoughts and masturbation? Do I have an attachment to any activity that is hurting my walk with God or my relationships? Am I using any behavior as a substitute for real intimacy with God or people? Is my number one temptation becoming my number one solution?...*

Ask: *Am I responsible for my success or is God? Am I better than other people? Is it hard for me to take advice from people? Am I a good listener? Am I in touch with the needs of those around me or aloof?* 📖

3. Take a few minutes to ask the Lord in prayer, "What can I do to set aside my idols and turn my face and heart totally toward You?"

By his mighty power at work within us, he is able to accomplish infinitely more than we could ever dare to ask or hope. (Ephesians 3:20, NLT)

📖 What's under the hood of your spiritual life? A kitty or a viper? Does your spiritual engine perform or sputter when you hit the throttle? Do you feel His power propelling you past your shortcomings, through your difficulties, and into health in your relationships? Or do you feel as if you're driving Auntie Eleanor's '64 Falcon stuck in first gear? God is looking for a full-throttle man—a man who worships God with his very life. 📖

Ah...Satisfied

Let's face it, a great ally in helping us stay focused on God is our contentment. I love how the apostle Paul showed contentment by accepting his life situations. There he was, locked up as a prisoner in Rome. He had a ton of reasons to be frustrated and unhappy, but you don't hear any whining from Brother Paul. Because of his gracious words, you can almost see the pleasant smile on his face and feel his deep satisfaction. This convict had to be about the freest dude in town!

> I rejoice greatly in the Lord that at last you have renewed your concern for me. Indeed, you have been concerned, but you had no opportunity to show it. I am not saying this because I am in need, for I have learned to be content whatever the circumstances. I know what it is to be in need, and I know what it is to have plenty. I have learned the secret of being content in any and every situation, whether well fed or hungry, whether living in plenty or in want. I can do everything through him who gives me strength. (Philippians 4:10–13)

We've often divorced that last sentence from the body of the thought, but what Paul is saying is that God's man becomes content because of the strength that comes with Christ's perspective. That perspective overcomes concern about your station in life. Both the love of affluence and loathing of poverty become null and void. God's man is free, whatever his situation, when he knows what is eternal.

1. What do you think caused Paul to be so content—regardless of his circumstances? Write down some specifics.

2. What situations in your life cause you to be most discontented?

Contentment…satisfaction…resting…connecting…giving…[sacrificing]. Do any of these come naturally to you? Me either. I need new desires. I need God to change my heart. I need to grow. I need to start risking the superficial for the supernatural.…

Comparison kills my contentment. The problem is, I have been trained to love new and to despise same.…

I hear the voice of the guy who does all the commercials ringing in my head. You know him. He starts convincing us by asking the same question over and over. "Aren't you tired of your old…" Broom? Dish soap? TV tray? Acne medication? Diet plan? Weed Wacker?

This is the hook and I'm the large-mouth bass.

3. To what extent do you feel your lack of contentment is fueled by advertising and the media? List some specific reasons for your answer.

___ very much
___ somewhat
___ not at all

📖 There have been times in my life when I have concentrated so much on what I don't have that I have failed to enjoy what I do have. During these times I was less joyful, discontent, and, to my shame, largely ungrateful. It's draining to be a man who always focuses on what he doesn't have, and in the process I stagnated spiritually.

On the other hand, I have had times of financial abundance as an executive, flush with financial bonuses, raises, and promotions. In those times, it was tempting to think that I was the author of my own success. I prayed less, became less dependent on God and more worldly in my focus. In both circumstances, I learned a lot about myself. Namely, that the issue wasn't the amount of money in my bank account, it was about what my character could and could not handle....

A poor man may focus on the spiritual gifts, ministry, and people he has influenced, and become spiritually rich. And the wealthy man may focus on stewarding his monetary affluence for God's purposes to also become spiritually rich. Contentment redefines "rich." Rich in God. Rich in relationships. Rich in living out His purposes wherever we are and in whatever we do. 📖

4. What has been your experience with finances—have you had greater satisfaction and contentment when you have less or more money? Why do you think this is true for you?

5. Jesus said, "No one can serve two masters. Either he will hate the one and love the other, or he will be devoted to the one and despise the other. You cannot serve both God and Money" (Matthew 6:24). Why do you think Jesus drew such a sharp line between serving God and serving money?

God's Mission

Ultimately, our ability to find and embrace contentment is just another factor in advancing God's cause. We are much more effective as God's men when our appetites are under control and our devotion and worship are directed solely to Him.

> 📖 We are here to complete a mission—His mission. There is a myth that God's man must reject and defeat in his own heart, the one that says: you are here to complete *your* mission. This is the Guadalcanal of the spiritual life—His plan or mine? The world and the devil offer us a menu of identities and connected missions that distract God's man from the original plan. Under these deceptions, we are free to use our resources as we choose. We're also free to complain in anger and bitterness about our losses and broken dreams.
>
> The turning point in this battle comes when we risk embracing God's purpose in what we lack. More specifically, when we allow our character to be shaped through contentment with less rather than constantly devoting our time, thoughts, and God-given talents to acquiring stuff. 📖

1. What would be your short description of God's plan for humanity?

2. What might your life look like if you were less distracted by acquiring stuff?

In God's plan, less does not necessarily mean poverty and more does not necessarily mean wealth—each represents something different to every man depending on his situation. However, contentment does mean that a condition of the heart that preserves God's best is happening in and through you wherever He has called you to be, and with whatever He has called you to have. That is why contentment means something unique to every man and is something every God's man is supposed to pray for.

3. What change in your thinking about wealth and possessions would make the greatest difference in the level of contentment you feel?

📖 It's good for us to say no to ourselves sometimes. It's good for us to say no to our kids versus promoting immediate gratification and impulsiveness in their character. It's a good thing for married couples to delay a big purchase, pause a day or two to pray and ask what God wants them to do with His money. It's good for me to say no to some things so I can say yes to God. This is risky business for men who live in a material world, but it is the right risk if you are God's man. We are called to be content. That means, in some cases we will be asked to delay or divert prosperity so that others may experience Jesus's love. 📖

4. If you are a husband and father, what are some things you can do to encourage more contentment among other family members?

As I described in *Risk,* one of my pastors once preached a great sermon on being thankful. He gave us a homework assignment of starting each day by thanking God for twenty-five things. Each day we were to add to the list. Man, after a few days I was stretching to fill my quota. But even though I ended up thanking God for things like nose drops, the process really helped me develop a more thankful, contented attitude.

"Give thanks in all circumstances, for this is God's will for you in Christ Jesus" (1 Thessalonians 5:18). Notice it doesn't say give thanks *for* everything but give thanks *in* everything.

This is a mystery to me. A self-sufficient or prideful heart fuels discontentedness and broken relationships with God and people. But gratitude leads to contentment if we are thankful as God commands.

Here's a helpful reality: it is impossible to be *thankfully* discontent.

5. I'll pass along my pastor's suggestion to you: start each day by making a list of twenty-five things you are thankful for. Maybe you can even make it a family project. Use the space provided here to get started.

Risk Management

Remember

> I know what it is to be in need, and I know what it is to have plenty. I have learned the secret of being content in any and every situation, whether well fed or hungry, whether living in plenty or in want. I can do everything through him who gives me strength. (Philippians 4:12–13)

Reflect

1. Just what would you say is Paul's secret to being content?

2. Are there challenges in your life that seem insurmountable? Based on this verse, what advice might the apostle Paul give you as you meet these challenges?

Respond

This week, compile a list of issues that have you discontented. Present each one to the Lord in prayer, and ask Him to help you use His strength in removing every item from that list—in His timing.

 Risk Assessment (Man to Man)

1. Talk about the issue of contentment. Take turns sharing three issues where you struggle to remain contented.
2. Share with each other three areas where you have great contentment.

3. As you wrap up in prayer, pray specifically for each other's needs in the area of contentment. Also give thanks to God for all that you are grateful for.

Risk and Reward (Small Group Discussion)

1. We know that Jesus was a passionate person. Want proof? Read this: "I know your deeds, that you are neither cold nor hot. I wish you were either one or the other! So, because you are lukewarm—neither hot nor cold—I am about to spit you out of my mouth" (Revelation 3:15–16). What might be some examples of lukewarm behavior among God's men? Why does there seem to be a tendency toward lukewarmness in so many Christians? In your experience, what are some good ways to keep devotion to Christ red hot?
2. What do you think the apostle Paul was getting at when he wrote, "Continue to work out your salvation with fear and trembling" (Philippians 2:12)?
3. In *Risk* I tell the story of two of my friends confronting me on some issues (see pages 84–87). Has anyone in the group ever been called on the carpet spiritually? Was it a positive or negative experience? What has been the result in your life?
4. This is a quote from *Risk:* "Polluting your worship of Christ is Satan's goal, and he will try to infect it by introducing worldly desires to increase, indulge, and impress." Have you experienced a connection between lack of passion in worship and involvement with things of the world? On a daily basis, in what ways are you aware of Satan's battle against you—his plan to steal, kill, and destroy (see John 10:10)?
5. What in your life tends to create the greatest amount of discontentment?
6. *Risk* lists some options that can lead to deeper satisfaction in life. Read this list—after each item ask those in the group to offer their thoughts on how contentment might be affected in each instance.

- risk contentment over consumption
- risk satisfaction over searching for more
- risk gratitude over meaningless gratification
- risk resting in what we have over restlessness in what we lack
- risk connecting with the Joneses over competing with them
- risk giving more money to God's work over getting a new toy
- risk careers for a cause
- risk having less on earth for more in heaven

7. Close this session by taking turns sharing what you are grateful to God for.

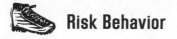

Risk Behavior

Here's what needs to happen before the next small group meeting:

1. Complete your personal study of session 4, which includes reading chapters 9, 10, and 11 in *Risk.*
2. Meet with your accountability partner.
3. Accomplish the Risk task you listed under Respond in the Risk Management section on page 58.
4. Record any of your observations in the Risk Journal.

Risk Journal

____

____

4

getting real

This week's session is based on chapter 9, "Achilles Heels," chapter 10, "Do You Have a Space Invader?" and chapter 11, "The Ruthless Way," in Risk.

We haven't been avoiding tough issues by any means, but in this session we will definitely cut to the quick. Our topics—honesty, sin, and accountability.

In what follows, you will see that these themes mesh well. The ruthless rooting out of sin requires personal honesty. And nothing can help keep you honest and on track spiritually quite like a quality accountability relationship with a space invader.

Risk Analysis

What is the most expensive mistake you have ever made? I'm not talking about losing a deal, buying a lemon at the auto dealer, or purchasing a home that started depreciating the day after you bought it. I am talking about mistakes that cost you in your relationships, took a toll on your physical and spiritual well-being, or exacted a price in your life that you're still paying today. What comes to mind?...

At times we all wonder why God allows us to experience such incredible pain. There seems to be no point in it. Whether it is something we did or something someone else did to us or something we had no control over, if we are willing to let Him use it, He can bring about His glory through our thorny issues we wish we didn't have to talk about. The best and most effective God's men are the ones who risk talking about their biggest source of shame or biggest obstacle they face as a man.

1. As you look back on your life, what are some of your whoppers—big mistakes you wish had never happened?

2. What are some of the hard-knock, valuable lessons you learned from your mistakes?

3. Have you ever had a friend or acquaintance tell you about some big personal mistake he made? How did his honesty affect you?

> God has lots of plans for our mistakes and weaknesses. It's counterintuitive to most men to think that way because our style is to hide them. So for a man to accept his failures, losses, and struggles as part of who he is (that is, reality), not things to be hidden away and ignored, is a big leap of faith. It's even more risky to allow God to use those same things to serve other people.

The incredible apostle Paul, that brilliant and tough-as-nails man who wrote much of the New Testament, had his share of challenges. Here's what he had to say about his weakness:

> So I wouldn't get a big head, I was given the gift of a handicap to keep me in constant touch with my limitations. Satan's angel did his best to get me down; what he in fact did was push me to my knees. No danger then of walking around high and mighty! At first I didn't think of it as a gift, and begged God to remove it. Three times I did that, and then he told me,
>
> My grace is enough; it's all you need.
> My strength comes into its own in your weakness.
>
> Once I heard that, I was glad to let it happen. I quit focusing on the handicap and began appreciating the gift. It was a case of Christ's strength moving in on my weakness. Now I take limitations in stride, and with good cheer, these limitations that cut me down to size—abuse, accidents, opposition, bad breaks. I just let Christ take over! And so the weaker I get, the stronger I become. (2 Corinthians 12:7–10, MSG)

> God's plan is to use the very things we want to keep a secret or keep hidden. In fact, one of the greatest things he wants to do is to bring us into the truth of reality to encourage others who are struggling with our same issues.

4. Can you recall a time when your sharing of a weakness or personal problem helped someone else? What were the results? If you've never done this, can you think of something God has taught you through tough times or pain that would benefit others?

Honesty Terrifies the Opposition

📖 The presence of the Evil One is a constant threat. With all the ways God could use your weaknesses and problems in the lives of others, you can believe the Enemy is going to throw out some major artillery to prevent you from facing those most sensitive areas and insecurities as a man. He wants you to minimize any weaknesses you might have, as though they don't really exist. Then you can get right back to relying on yourself....

God's power and strength will invade your authenticity, and you will become real to those who are fake and dangerous to those looking for safety. Authenticity always leads to credibility (everybody loves someone strong enough to be honest), which leads to vulnerability and trust. 📖

1. Why do you think Satan would not want you to be honest about struggles in your life?

2. Can you think of someone in your life now who would be encouraged to know that you have struggled with issues similar to those he's facing? Pray for an opportunity to appropriately come alongside this brother (or sister) in the Lord.

Invading Your Space

I know it sounds a bit weird, but I see myself as a spiritual mechanic of men. And a quick way I have to check on how a guy's spiritual engine is running is to get a reading on his relationships with other men. I find this to be the oil of spiritual growth in a man's life. If he's down a quart or two on accountability, I know his motor is running hot and working too hard to maintain performance. And all parts of his life are affected—in particular, his relationships.

The best way I know of to keep a man's spiritual life humming like a BMW is to make sure his space is invaded by at least one other godly man through an accountability relationship. Like most men, I had to learn this the hard way.

> I can't believe how long I was a Christian and never once encountered a man who cared enough to get in my space over obvious issues. Maybe the Christians I hung around with didn't feel I needed to be shaken down. As a consequence, I was winning the battle of images and masks while losing the war for character and Christlikeness. Part of it was definitely me. I was afraid, very, very afraid for people to know the dark side, the struggling side, and the wounds in my character. Letting someone see under my body armor might mean bugged-out eyeballs

and deep gasping for air. But the other part of it was the men in my life who did not know what real accountability looked like and who, too, were afraid of showing their sores for the sake of Christ. 📖

1. How often in your life has another man shown significant interest in getting in your space over obvious issues? If never or not very often, why do you think that's the case?

2. How open are you to having your personal space invaded by someone who wants to help you grow in Christ?

📖 Spiritual independence is an oxymoron. The key word here is *moron.*

"My relationship with God is personal" is a common refrain. I hear this from men who don't have the spine to accept responsibility or to admit a fault, or both.…

Listen closely to how Paul managed the news and responded to the men in Thessalonica who might have been feeling as if they had the Jesus thing wired.

"Finally, brothers, we instructed you how to live in order to please God, as in fact you are living. Now we ask you and urge you in the Lord Jesus to do this more and more. For you know what instructions we gave you by the authority of the Lord Jesus.

"It is God's will that you should be sanctified: that you should avoid sexual immorality; that each of you should learn to control his own body in a way that is holy and honorable, not in passionate lust like the heathen, who do not know God; and that in this matter no one should wrong his brother or take advantage of him. The Lord will punish men for all such sins, as we have already told you and warned you." (1 Thessalonians 4:1–6)....

If I were a Thessalonian believer, I might push back and get in Paul's face. "What authority do you have to get into my business? Isn't that between me and the Lord?" Paul knows this, and that is why he says, "We ask you, we urge you in the Lord Jesus...by the authority of the Lord Jesus." In other words, "In the Lord Jesus, *your* business *is* my business and *my* business is your business."

3. Do you agree or disagree that "spiritual independence is an oxymoron"? Why?

4. In America and throughout much of the world, being independent and self-sufficient is highly valued. How do such cultural ideas conflict with allowing others to look at our business and vice versa?

Most Christian men are unexamined, unknown, unconfessed, and unable to risk transparency for the sake of growth. It's tough to watch men—especially leaders—whose influence exceeds their unchecked character issues. God has to bench them, retrain them, and rebuild them....

Fellowship with other men will get you only so far. I know lots of guys in men's groups who are still the same guys with the same character producing the same problems year after year. They haven't narrowed their group down to one or two men and *expressed* the need for the next level of accountability to them—the kind that has teeth that bite hard and leave a mark. Listen to King David describe his desire to please God and his need for space invaders—guys close enough to knock him on his can! "Let a righteous man strike me—it is a kindness; let him rebuke me—it is oil on my head. My head will not refuse it" (Psalm 141:5). David knew he needed a real male friend, not a fan.

5. Why would David say that having a "righteous man strike me" was a good thing, an act of kindness?

6. Can you recall an incident or two in your life where another man's rebuke or valid criticism really helped you? Recall the details here.

Sometimes it's risky to present ourselves for examination because we know what it will involve....

[But] all of us need to get over the fear of being known. We need to take a step of faith and embrace *aggressive* accountability before it's too late....

Are you getting looked at regularly by at least one other man who doesn't care about your image, doesn't read your press clippings, and doesn't buy your spin? This man who cares about you becoming God's man needs full permission to examine, press, and push. He has an eye for Christlikeness and a sniper's rifle trained on your pride.

7. Why is living an examined life a risk?

8. What qualities would you look for in a man who might be a candidate to be your space invader (accountability partner)?

9. If you do not have an accountability relationship with a godly man, are you ready now to seek one out? Are you willing to give your time in such a relationship with a brother who is less mature spiritually than yourself? Write down specific answers to both questions.

Seek and Destroy the Bad Stuff

Obviously, a major reason for being honest about your own life and seeking the spiritual support of a godly man-brother is to confront and eradicate sin.

> 🕮 *Ruthlessness* is a term usually reserved for tyrants and insecure dictators. The Hitlers or Husseins of history. Yet, spiritually speaking, there is a tyrant who lives inside us all that must be spared no mercy. He is not to be managed. He is to be eliminated by our cooperation with God's Spirit on a daily basis....
>
> This battle against indwelling sin resembles the complexities of the War on Terror. First of all, intelligence is critical. The Enemy is shifty, hidden, networked, armed, and patient, and he knows you are after him. He can employ disguises, disinformation, and poisonous deception to keep you at bay. He's got powerful allies (namely, the media-soaked culture and the devil) supplying him with ammunition.
>
> An Every Man Ministries poll reveals the predominant masculine sins

that need to be constantly tracked down reside in one or more of the following areas....

- lust or fantasy sex
- pride
- unresolved marital disconnection or infidelity
- materialism
- anger or resentments
- busyness or workaholism
- unforgiveness
- selfishness
- jealousy or envy
- impatience
- comparison
- spiritual apathy 📖

1. Run through this list of masculine sins. Which ones are you struggling with the most? Be honest. This is for your good!

2. Through your past experience, what ways of confronting personal sin have been most effective?

There is a method for getting after sin. I call it the ruthless way, which I have condensed here from *Risk:*

1. *We ask God to reveal sin directly to us.* "Search me, O God, and know my heart; test me and know my anxious thoughts. See if there is any offensive way in me, and lead me in the way everlasting" (Psalm 139:23–24).
2. *We place ourselves under the microscope of Scripture.* "I will walk about in freedom, for I have sought out your precepts" (Psalm 119:45).
3. *We allow other God's men to freely use the microscope.* "It is better to heed a wise man's rebuke than to listen to the song of fools" (Ecclesiastes 7:5).
4. *We ask our wives (if we're married) to be forward observers in our lives.* "Her husband has full confidence in her and lacks nothing of value. She brings him good, not harm, all the days of her life" (Proverbs 31:11–12).
5. *We kill sin by the piercing vision of the Holy Spirit.* "The Lord is the Spirit, and where the Spirit of the Lord is, there is freedom" (2 Corinthians 3:17).

3. Why do you think reading, studying, memorizing, meditating on, and discussing Scripture is so critical in the battle to eradicate your sin?

4. Why do we need the power of the Holy Spirit to ultimately win against sin?

Our sins were not forgiven so that we may casually and contentedly continue in them. Viewing sin seriously, seeking freedom from its bondage, and vigilantly dealing with it is the ongoing preoccupation of God's man. If we aren't dutiful to kill sin, we're abusers of God's grace, which incidentally did not come cheap.

5. As you continue your spiritual journey, how might you be sure that dealing with sin is your personal preoccupation?

There is no final elimination of sin for the believer on earth. Though the Bible is crystal clear there is to be a steady weakening of it through our constant fight, with increasing evidence of frequent success, the final victory will go to the Savior. Through His indwelling power, we can be assured that every effort expended will be rewarded.

Brothers, we have an obligation—but it is not to the sinful nature, to live according to it. For if you live according to the sinful nature, you will die; but if by the Spirit you put to death the misdeeds of the body, you will live, because those who are led by the Spirit of God are sons of God. (Romans 8:12–14)

Risk Management

Remember

> Search me, O God, and know my heart; test me and know my anxious thoughts. See if there is any offensive way in me, and lead me in the way everlasting. (Psalm 139:23–24)

Reflect

1. What are your ways of letting God "search [you]" and "know [your] heart"?

2. Go to the Lord in prayer and simply ask Him, *Is there some offensive way in me that I need to know about so that I can repent?* Wait and listen for His response. If He doesn't communicate immediately, keep listening. He will show you.

Respond

During the coming week, with the assistance of the Holy Spirit, be on the lookout for areas of your life where you are not being honest. Make note of what you learn, and share your findings with your accountability partner.

 Risk Assessment (Man to Man)

1. Take turns in telling how the past week has gone. Ask each other, In what areas in your life do you struggle to be honest?
2. Take turns running through the checklist below. Do not use this as a legalistic club to wound each other. Reviewing these items provides a type of maintenance checklist on a man's spiritual condition. Are you:
   - spending time in the Word and prayer?
   - accountable and sexually pure?
   - committed to wife and family?
   - serving the Lord?
   - seeking to please the Lord in all things?

- sharing your faith?
- working with other men?
- tithing and giving?
- leading in your church?
- pursuing ministry opportunities?
- visibly living out God's purposes?

Continue to work out your salvation with fear and trembling, for it is God who works in you to will and to act according to his good purpose. (Philippians 2:12–13)

Risk and Reward (Small Group Discussion)

1. Why does God allow us to make mistakes and have pain in life?
2. Why do men seem to have trouble admitting they have faults, make mistakes, don't have all the answers?
3. What is the big problem with having blind spots?
4. What would you say to a guy who had some obvious sin issues but told you, "Stay out of my business. My walk with God is personal"?
5. Quickly review the story of David and Nathan in 2 Samuel 12. What does this incident reveal about how God uses other men to help us stay on track spiritually?
6. My pastor, Rick Warren, says, "Sin is fun for a season. You have your kicks. Then you have your kickbacks." What kind of kickbacks has sin had in your life?
7. To cut to the bottom line—why is it so important as men to constantly detect and eradicate sin from our lives?

 Risk Behavior

Here's what needs to happen before the next small group meeting:

1. Complete your personal study of session 5, which includes reading chapters 12 and 13 in *Risk.*
2. Meet with your accountability partner.
3. Accomplish the Risk task you listed under Respond in the Risk Management section on page 77.
4. Record any of your observations in the Risk Journal.

Risk Journal

5

game on

This week's session is based on chapter 12, "The Highest Vision, the Noblest Goal," and chapter 13, Spiritual Ebola," in Risk.

The kingdom of God needs more men who will leave the sidelines of their Christian life and get out on the field. I love what Dr. Tony Evans, the great pastor in Dallas, Texas, once said: "We don't need more Christians, we've got plenty of Christians. We need more disciples."

Tony wasn't implying that we should stop sharing the gospel and introducing others to Christ. He was taking aim at spiritual apathy and the unwillingness of so many Christians to sacrifice comfort for commitment to Jesus.

Are you tired of endless warmup drills and sitting on the bench in a uniform that never gets any grass stains? Do you want to make some plays and help the team win?

Game on!

Risk Analysis

There is a long tradition of God's leaders encouraging God's men to live out God's purposes single-mindedly. Jesus told His men of His upcoming suffering at the cross and then used that reality to motivate them. He was honest and clear. His men would have to reject other pursuits, carry the responsibility of God's man, and follow Him loyally to the end. He modeled for us how to call men to a mission. The call to the multitudes was different than the charge to His men.

"Then Jesus said to his disciples, 'If anyone would come after me, he must deny himself and take up his cross and follow me' " (Matthew 16:24).

1. Review the stories of what happened when Jesus chose His disciples. (See Matthew 4:18–22; Mark 2:14; Luke 4:38–5:11, and John 1:35–51.) What details in these stories stand out or are most surprising to you?

2. What do you think these first disciples were feeling as they heard and responded to Jesus's call to join Him?

In the early church, the relationship that the apostle Paul had with his protégé, Timothy, presents a detail-rich model of how one God's man trains, coaches, and encourages another, less seasoned God's man.

📖 Read the following as Timothy might have, receiving a scroll from a prison cell in Rome to you in ancient Greece. This will be your last communication from the man who led you to Christ, who trained you in the field, and who now awaits his execution. You read the first part of the note, which conveys encouragement to be faithful, and then you read: "You then, my son, be strong in the grace that is in Christ Jesus. And the things you have heard me say in the presence of many witnesses entrust to reliable men who will also be qualified to teach others" (2 Timothy 2:1–2). 📖

3. Why do you think Paul—before giving Timothy detailed instructions on ministry—puts such an emphasis on the grace of the Lord Jesus?

4. From just this one sentence (beginning with "And the things"), what specific insights do you gain into Paul's approach to mentoring?

Paul has more to say to Timothy—and us:

> Endure hardship with us like a good soldier of Christ Jesus. No one serving as a soldier gets involved in civilian affairs—he wants to please his commanding officer. Similarly, if anyone competes as an athlete, he does not receive the victor's crown unless he competes according to the rules. The hardworking farmer should be the first to receive a share of the crops. Reflect on what I am saying, for the Lord will give you insight into all this. (2 Timothy 2:3–7)

📖 Paul knew he had just dropped a bomb on Timothy that would require some heavy reflection. "Pause," he advised. "Think deeply and continuously on what I just said. This is a biggie." Timothy was going to have to take on a single identity, passion, and goal. He would have to train hard, work hard, and focus on results. The examples of commitment Paul meant were not weak wafflers. They were strong men with strong inner convictions who were willing to forgo comfort and discipline themselves to get results consistent with their identities. 📖

5. Outside of your spiritual life, what commitments have demanded the most from you?

6. In following Jesus, have you experienced the same urgency, focus, passion, intensity, extreme effort, and so on, that you did in these other pursuits? What are the reasons for differences or similarities?

📖 All these profiles fit Jesus's commitment call perfectly. All three deny themselves comfort for their journeys. All three accept responsibility. They pick up their crosses, move forward, and take action to stay loyal, compete, and work hard. All are noble in their own ways, Paul says, but Timothy has to think hard on the implications for his life. If he does, God will spell it out for him. 📖

7. Much like Paul asked Timothy to "reflect on what I am saying," I would like you to pause and think about the cost to follow Jesus as true, "leave it all on the field" disciples. Take as much time as you need—now and in the coming days—to answer this question: Are you willing to pay the price of authentic discipleship?

Being and Doing

📖 Paul had two goals for Timothy, and they are the same ones I have for you: that you would be strong and that you would risk making an impact. One is for your spiritual character. The other is for your actions for Christ. One is being; the other is doing. When both come together, you have a powerful witness for Him.

1. Why is it so important that a disciple of Christ be concerned about both his character and his actions?

To stay focused as God's men, we must tap the strength of God's grace. Picking his strategy carefully, Paul gave Timothy the secret to a long-lasting witness for Jesus Christ: grace. What saved us is also what sustains us as God's men. If we focus on the love and forgiveness we were given, we become unstoppable for God. No doubt, no fear, no regret. No opinion or prideful thinking can overpower our witness.

2. What does God's grace mean to you? How would you define it to someone who had never heard about grace?

3. Why is it important not just to be saved by grace but to live by grace?

4. Are there rewards for Christ's faithful disciples? (See 2 Timothy 2:6 and 12, as examples.)

Even Jesus had a reward in mind when He was completing His mission on earth:

> Let us fix our eyes on Jesus, the author and perfecter of our faith, who for the joy set before him endured the cross, scorning its shame, and sat down at the right hand of the throne of God. (Hebrews 12:2)

> 📖 Like Timothy, God's men need this tactical reminder to stay focused and persevere. Some days will be harder than others, but God is pleased with His soldier, He rewards His champion, and He brings abundant harvest to His hard-working servant....
>
> Brother, nothing is more worth your sacrifice than the Greatest Commandment and the Great Commission. 📖

Invest Wisely

Here's another installment in Paul's basic training course with Timothy:

> What you heard from me, keep as the pattern of sound teaching, with faith and love in Christ Jesus. Guard the good deposit that was entrusted to you—guard it with the help of the Holy Spirit who lives in us. (2 Timothy 1:13–14)

When it came to being a disciple, the apostle Paul looked at the men he touched much like banks that have been entrusted with the valuable commodities of his spiritual investments. While held prisoner in Rome by the emperor Nero, Paul made sure one of his best trainees remembered how precious the investment of his life was to him. The trainee, Timothy, was a spiritual repository of Paul's best thinking, modeling, ministry. And message. These needed to be both guarded and preserved by Timothy as well as multiplied like an investment into the lives of others.

1. What is the "good deposit" that Christ, godly teachers, mentors, and friends have entrusted to you?

2. What can you do to guard this good deposit from being abused, misused, lost, or stolen? What's the role of the Holy Spirit in assisting you?

After making a commitment to value and safeguard the message and truth deposited into his life, Timothy needed to take one more step: give it away to other men and multiply his impact generationally for Christ. Just a few sentences later in this same letter, he is told not just to guard the deposit but to *make deposits* in the lives of other men....

It was gonna take some thinking, but the call was crystal clear: "Reproduce yourself, Timothy."

3. Why do you think so many Christians seem to falter at this point—they don't move on from being grateful recipients of God's grace and goodness to become active agents in seeing that others receive God's grace?

4. On a scale of 1 to 10 (1 being "whispering wimp" to 10 being "raging reproducer"), how would you rate your performance as a reproducer of Christ's disciples? Give reasons for your rating.

Born to Reproduce

> 🕮 Paul defined discipleship in the simplest and most functional sense: it's taking another man on a spiritual journey with you. He grabbed Timothy, took him for outpatient surgery, and hit the road! Those early days must have been flooding Timothy's mind as he read Paul's letter penned from a dungeon in Rome. They traveled together, taught together, ate many a meal together, laughed I'm sure, saw a huge number of people come to know Jesus personally. 🕮

1. In your own spiritual journey, do you have a "Paul"—someone who purposefully mentored you in how to become a God's man? Whether you have such a man in your life or not, what have been the spiritual results for you?

If you never were mentored, *it's not too late!* And even if you were, you still need ongoing training. I think a good model for each of us is to always have at least two men in our lives: one is a more mature God's man who is helping us grow; the second is a less mature God's man into whom we are pouring ourselves. (And of course one of these—or a spiritual peer—needs to be your accountability partner.)

> 🕮 Outbreaks of viral infections like Ebola need to be contained, but good infections, spiritual ones, do not. In fact, Jesus's own life reflected intentional infection with His men—it was needed and necessary if God's plan for the world was to be successful. His life came into close personal contact with ordi-

nary men. Out of the thousands, He intentionally selected and associated with twelve disciples and infected eleven....

"Everyone, after he has been fully trained, will be like his teacher" (Luke 6:40, NASB), Jesus told his trainees. His end game was infection. His actions were deliberate, and He wanted His men to possess His mission, share His feelings on things, and imitate His behavior. His way was God's way, and that was what made Him confident and contagious....

Jesus knew that the measure of His mission would be His ability to reproduce Himself. Otherwise the mission would not get done.

Fact time: God's man is made to reproduce. 📖

2. Why is it important that the sharing of the gospel and the reproducing of men of faith be so intentional and personal?

3. Jesus took His trainees with Him everywhere. How do you think this 24/7, hands-on learning approach might look in the reproduction of disciples today?

📖 Risking reproducing yourself spiritually requires guts and perseverance, but it is also the greatest adventure God's man will ever take. Raising up and training a leader to do God's work is nuclear—it has a blast zone that extends to people you will never know you impacted. All because you invested yourself and made deposits into the life of one other person and intentionally brought him to maturity in order to release him to ministry. People touching people...who touch people...for Jesus in a chain of relationships that spans *centuries.*

Risk Management

Remember

He said to them, "Go into all the world and preach the good news to all creation." (Mark 16:15)

Reflect

1. This Remember scripture is often quoted to encourage missionary activity around the globe—which it does. But where does "the world" begin for each of us?

2. It's decision time. In prayer, ask the Holy Spirit to help you answer three questions, giving reasons for your answers, if possible:

    - Who is on my radar that needs to hear the gospel from me?

- Who is—or might become—my spiritual mentor?

- Who is—or might become—my spiritual disciple?

Respond

This week, take action related to each of the answers you just recorded in the Reflect section. Even if they are just baby steps, what will you do to begin the process of sharing the good news with a specific person, reconfirming or locating a spiritual mentor, and identifying a spiritual disciple? Record your specific objectives here.

 Risk Assessment (Man to Man)

Recap for each other the details of your spiritual journey in the past week.

1. Each of you, give a summary of your individual experience being disciples. How has it gone? In what areas are you strong? What areas need more work?

2. Take turns sharing your specific goals related to communicating the gospel to others, being discipled, and discipling another man in the faith. Commit these desires and requests to God in prayer.

Risk and Reward (Small Group Discussion)

1. The book *Risk* contains the following list of what Jesus deposited in his disciples (page 175). Have someone read the list out loud. Then have individuals explain what various items on the list mean to them personally. Are there other things Jesus gave that are not mentioned on this list?
   - Himself—all that He was and was not
   - His connection to and experiences with the Father
   - His insight into God's Word and life
   - His grace and acceptance
   - His goals and vision
   - His inspiration and encouragement
   - His personal call to godliness
   - His humanity and vulnerability as a man
   - His teaching gifts
   - His leadership skills
   - His "out of the box" approaches to situations
   - His compassion for the lost
   - His passion for God's purposes
   - His spiritual spine in the face of intimidation
   - His willingness to go against the culture in order to be God's man
   - His sense of people, their needs, and how to meet them
   - His ministry of teaching, preaching, healing, and sharing God's love

- His authority and commission
- His willingness to sacrifice

2. Are there ways that Christians abuse God's grace? Explain why you agree or disagree.
3. The topic of this lesson has been making disciples. In your journey as a Christian, what has encouraged you to be a better disciple? What has been a source of discouragement?
4. In *Risk* there's a passage that reads: "The most natural and positive thing for a man is to reproduce. God made us that way. Think about it. Why do you think we are consciously and subconsciously driven by our sexual impulses? We seek to connect, reproduce, procreate, and multiply!… The problem is that men don't translate their natural drive to reproduce into a spiritual reproduction, because sin and fear have conflicted and polluted our desires." Do you agree that men are natural reproducers? If so, can we apply this natural inclination to spiritual reproduction? What are the ramifications of this?
5. What factors keep men from being discipled?
6. What factors keep men from discipling others?
7. How can God's men help each other grow in the arena of discipleship?

Risk Behavior

Here's what needs to happen before the next small group meeting:

1. Complete your personal study of session 6, which includes reading chapter 14 in *Risk.*
2. Meet with your accountability partner.

3. Accomplish the Risk task you listed under Respond in the Risk Management section on page 93.
4. Record any of your observations in the Risk Journal.

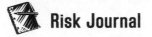

Risk Journal

6

godly "gut feel"

This week's session is based on chapter 14, "The First Two Seconds," in Risk.

We all have said or heard the old expression, "In the blink of an eye." It's true that wonderful and horrible events can occur—just that *quick.* In his book *Blink,* Malcolm Gladwell demonstrates how often superior, reliable judgments can be made in "the first two seconds" of evaluation. Wow! Now I understand why I can rattle off my order at Starbucks at lightning speed!

As good as we might get at making snap decisions, though, as a God's man, we possess something even more remarkable: living inside of us is a fathomless Source of wisdom and guidance. How can we make full use of such an incredible asset?

Let's check it out.

Risk Analysis

In his book *Blink,* author Malcolm Gladwell bravely points out that great decisions come about by an ability we all have to quickly filter out the most meaningful factors from the irrelevant. He calls it "rapid cognition" and "thin-slicing." We might call it a gut feeling or a guiding instinct. If you read his stuff, you are going to feel validated as a man, even euphoric, because he validates the masculine way of decision making—my style of decision making—quick!...

These "thin slices" help us take charge in the first two seconds of any given situation. The big question for all of us is: what is the substance of our experiences and environments that guides us in these critical moments? What's filtering our reactions and responses? Can we trust it to help us as God's men? 📖

1. What's your go-to style of decision making?

___ lightning quick
___ extended analysis
___ depends on the situation

Regardless of your response, one thing is sure: we need as much of God's wisdom as we can assemble to make good choices. I love how Jesus dealt with the decisions He faced:

📖 Jesus was a man who demonstrated that He could think on His feet. The Gospels reveal a man who could sift through a situation, person, or mob, throw out all that was irrelevant, and target the core issue or necessary action. His answers to things were not exhaustive, and His methods were unorthodox at times, but they were always consistent with His goals and mission as the Son of God. Above all, He never panicked in the face of pressure or wavered in the moment. He was grace and truth. He was silk and, when needed, steel. 📖

2. Why do you think Jesus was so brilliant and skilled in dealing with such a wide variety of circumstances?

📖 Both Jesus's private life and public life were loaded with moments that required special intuition and efficient, God-honoring responses. Sound familiar?

- confrontations with the competition
- personal temptations when emotionally and physically weak
- interruptions in your workflow
- comparison to others
- badgering and harassment
- people placed on your porch with big life issues and problems
- dysfunctional family blowups
- needing to speak the truth when it's going to sting the other person 📖

3. Are you dealing with situations similar to the ones listed above? What insights, based on how Jesus approached His challenges, can help you face yours?

📖 What we clearly see is a man whose experiences, exposures, and environments had created an intuition He could trust and that performed. His relationship with

His Father, His understanding of His purposes, His encounters with real needs of people, His investments of time and energy in the disciples, His service to others, and His strong sense of identity made Him free and successful in spontaneous situations. When called upon to improvise, Jesus thrived because He had a strong adherence to a simple framework: love God and love people. He was free under pressure because He was committed to never denying loyalty and love for His Father and serving people. "My food...is to do the will of him who sent me" (John 4:34) and the "Son of Man did not come to be served, but to serve" (Mark 10:45) are the kinds of statements coming from the mouth of the God-Man that reflect the general character of His experiences and environments that shaped His intuition at any given moment. 📖

On a Mission

📖 I encourage men around the world to risk becoming purpose-driven men who arrange their lives around:

- knowing and loving God
- connecting to other God's men
- becoming like Christ
- having a ministry to believers
- reaching out to those without Christ 📖

1. If you have (or would like to have) a mission statement for your life, what key ideas does it include? How do the points in your mission statement resemble or differ from the five items listed above?

📖 Men who are committed to arranging their lives around these purposes are free in the fight because God's way eliminates confusion and provides clear decisions and godly instincts for effectiveness.

Whether you're sizing up a decision, a relationship, or a particular circumstance, God's man, devoted fully to God's purposes, will not need a long list of options. Instead, he will target what really matters based on his exposure and experiences with God's purposes. 📖

2. What are some ways you could train your intuition in a healthy way?

3. How would you define "godly instincts"?

When as God's men we are aligned with what God desires for us, that is, *obedient,* then we will see issues clearly and much of the time instinctively choose the following:

___ loyalty to God over man
___ connection over isolation
___ character of Christ over comfort

___ serving God's people over self
___ speaking up about Christ's work in his life over remaining silent
___ the principles in the Word over those of the world
___ the Spirit's voice over the flesh's lures

4. What kind of a grade would you give yourself on how you respond to the above choices? It might be helpful to grade A through F on each item, then assign a total grade. Don't succumb to pride or guilt—just honestly evaluate yourself. Ask the Holy Spirit to give you insight. (And no grading on the curve!)

5. Having done this evaluation, what areas in your spiritual life appear to need more attention?

📖 A man who risks committing himself fully to these purposes, consciously builds his life around them, and keeps punching will not be mastered by any earthly moment. He might get stunned or knocked down, but he will come out punching and land more blows. 📖

6. It is good for us to remember and give thanks for victories in the Christian life. List several incidents where you followed any of these purposes on the list above and saw God bless and move. Give Him thanks and the glory for each one!

Guided by the Spirit

📖 Holy hunches. Sensing the Spirit. Trusting insight over eyesight. All this talk sounds ethereal and spooky to a lot of men because it requires faith—and risk. If you are God's man, Gladwell's research confirms what you should already know—God's Spirit is not failing in your life. In fact, He is constantly providing direction and communication. The problem is not with Him; it's with us. God speaks to our minds and provides opportunities for spiritual rapid cognition. 📖

1. How do you respond to the statement, God's Spirit "is constantly providing direction and communication"? Is that your experience?

> But when he, the Spirit of truth, comes, he will guide you into all truth. He will not speak on his own; he will speak only what he hears, and he will tell you what is yet to come. (John 16:13)

2. In what ways does the Holy Spirit speak to you?

3. How might you change any thought patterns and actions that would make it more likely you will hear the Holy Spirit and clearly receive His guidance?

Just Say Yes

Every God's man desperately wants to connect with God and clearly understand what His desires are. There is nothing, ultimately, that can prevent this! But we must want to have this level of communication and create a personal environment that cranks up the receptivity of our spiritual antenna. That's where we turn to the Holy Spirit. Isn't God amazing? He has provided inside each of us the total answer to our desire to communicate with the Father—the Holy Spirit!

> I will ask the Father, and he will give you another Counselor to be with you forever—the Spirit of truth. The world cannot accept him, because it neither sees

> him nor knows him. But you know him, for he lives with you and will be in you. (John 14:16–17)
>
> Don't you know that you yourselves are God's temple and that God's Spirit lives in you? (1 Corinthians 3:16)

So just how do we make sure that we are saying yes to the Holy Spirit? Here's my action plan (slightly condensed) from *Risk* for making that happen:

1. *Desire to please God.* The bottom line of all spiritual progress begins here. "No more stumbling around. Get on with it! The good, the right, the true—these are the actions appropriate for daylight hours. Figure out what will please Christ, and then do it" (Ephesians 5:8–10, MSG).
2. *Recognize and surrender to His role in your life on an increasing basis.* "So, as the Holy Spirit says: 'Today, if you hear his voice, do not harden your hearts,' " wrote the author of Hebrews to early Christians who are about to make a big mistake in their walk with the Lord (3:7–8). There's nothing confusing here: that voice telling you to do it God's way instead of your way is the Holy Spirit!
3. *Go under His influence now.* Prayer is how God's man initiates, activates, and applies the Holy Spirit's abilities in his life. Sincerely read this prayer expressing your desire to go under the control of the Spirit, and pray it earnestly and often: *Holy Spirit, I know I need You. I know that I am tempted to be in control of my life, and when I am, I miss out on Your wonderful plan. I am sorry for taking over when I shouldn't or muting Your voice so that I can sin. I surrender. Take control of my life right now and fill me. Speak to me loudly, lead me, guide me, open my eyes to God's plan, and help me choose it quickly. Thank You for taking control. In Jesus's name I ask. Amen.*

4. *Recognize that discomfort is the Holy Spirit signaling you to make a choice for God.* The role of the Holy Spirit in the life of God's man is to make him uneasy and uncomfortable when there is a choice on the line for self versus God. When anything can take your relationships with God and people into a pit, the Holy Spirit will automatically flood your mind with warnings, passages of Scripture, people, or circumstances designed to give you a spiritual fever.
5. *Take right actions in spite of feeling.* The key to winning moments is the first few seconds. Prompt (versus delayed) obedience is critical. When we obey without listening to conflicting feelings, we are trusting God. When I'm camping with my kids and I see something dangerous they don't, I call their name, call them over, and explain after. I expect them to listen to my voice over their feelings about continuing their own way. Because there is a trust there, they do an about-face when I call. That's why the Bible tells God's man to pay close attention, trust, and keep the communication channels wide open: "Since we live by the Spirit, let us keep in step with the Spirit" (Galatians 5:25).

Let's review the bullet points of my action plan for saying yes to the Holy Spirit:

- desire to please God
- recognize and surrender to His role in your life on an increasing basis
- go under His influence now
- recognize that discomfort is the Holy Spirit signaling you to make a choice for God
- take right actions in spite of feeling

Now, use the following questions to help refine your own action plan for quick, efficient, and godly responsiveness to the Holy Spirit:

1. How do you know what is pleasing to God?

2. List several attitudes and/or practices that will help you surrender more quickly and completely to the nudging communication of the Holy Spirit.

3. If you do not go under His influence on a daily basis, frequently acknowledge your need for the Holy Spirit's guidance, and ask Him to take control—in the name of Jesus.

4. How do you know when the Holy Spirit is using discomfort to alert you and help you make a good choice that honors God? Are there any issues of discomfort in your life now awaiting a good decision on your part?

5. How good or bad are you at setting feelings aside appropriately and, in faith, just doing what God wants?

Risk Management

Remember

The Counselor, the Holy Spirit, whom the Father will send in my name, will teach you all things and will remind you of everything I have said to you. (John 14:26)

Reflect

1. Based on what Jesus said in this verse, how involved should the Holy Spirit be in your life? Is this happening with you now?

2. Think about how you have or have not cooperated with the Holy Spirit in your spiritual journey. What changes should you make to allow the Holy Spirit greater freedom to work in your life?

Respond

In the coming week, on a daily basis write down somewhere (here or using the journal pages of this workbook) how you have heard the Holy Spirit and what you did as a result. You will be surprised and amazed at how often—when you listen carefully—God is speaking to you through the Holy Spirit.

 Risk Assessment (Man to Man)

1. Enjoy some time discussing what has gone on with each of you in the past week. Treasure this opportunity to fellowship, to bear one another's burdens, to offer encouragement, to challenge, and—above all—to grow stronger in Christ with the help of a godly man who is a fellow soldier in your band of brothers.
2. Alternate in sharing a few of your individual experiences in having the Holy Spirit guide, comfort, nudge, whisper, shout, lead, and so on, in various situations. If one of you is having trouble hearing the Holy Spirit, talk about that, too.
3. Close in prayer.

 Risk and Reward (Small Group Discussion)

1. This statement occurs in *Risk:* "Good decisions do not require great deliberation." Do you agree or disagree? Why?
2. The book *Risk* discusses how Jesus "owned the first two seconds of any situation." Take a few minutes to discuss how Jesus showed such great insight—quickly and decisively—in each of these situations:
   - *When put on the spot by those seeking to trap him spiritually...* "One of them, an expert in the law, tested him with this question: 'Teacher, which is the greatest commandment in the Law?' Jesus replied, ' "Love the Lord your God with all your heart and with all your soul and with all your mind." This is the first and greatest commandment. And the second is like it: "Love your neighbor as yourself." All the Law and the Prophets hang on these two commandments' " (Matthew 22:35–40).

- *When put on the spot by the devil's proposition...* "The devil said to him, 'If you are the Son of God, tell this stone to become bread.' Jesus answered, 'It is written: "Man does not live on bread alone" ' " (Luke 4:3–4).
- *When put on the spot by a mob holding a woman caught in the act of adultery...* " 'Teacher, this woman was caught in the act of adultery. In the Law Moses commanded us to stone such women. Now what do you say?' They were using this question as a trap, in order to have a basis for accusing him. But Jesus bent down and started to write on the ground with his finger. When they kept on questioning him, he straightened up and said to them, 'If any one of you is without sin, let him be the first to throw a stone at her' " (John 8:4–7).
- *When put on the spot in the middle of a family conflict...* "Martha was distracted by all the preparations that had to be made. She came to him and asked, 'Lord, don't you care that my sister has left me to do the work by myself? Tell her to help me!' 'Martha, Martha,' the Lord answered, 'you are worried and upset about many things, but only one thing is needed. Mary has chosen what is better, and it will not be taken away from her' " (Luke 10:40–42).

3. What principles for responding to situations and making decisions are found in these examples from Jesus's life?
4. What examples from your own life reveal either good or bad results from decisions made intuitively and rapidly?
5. As God's men, we have a built-in source of wisdom and understanding in the Holy Spirit. In your day-to-day life, how aware are you of the Holy Spirit's guidance?
6. Share some examples from your personal experience of situations where you heard what the Holy Spirit was saying and obeyed. What were the results?
7. This session's Remember scripture is John 14:26: "The Counselor, the Holy Spirit, whom the Father will send in my name, will teach you all things and will

remind you of everything I have said to you." Since this is such an incredible promise to provide knowledge and wisdom, how can we increase the role of the Holy Spirit in every aspect of our lives?

Risk Behavior

Here's what needs to happen before the next small group meeting:

1. Complete your personal study of session 7, which includes reading chapters 15 and 16 in *Risk.*
2. Meet with your accountability partner.
3. Accomplish the Risk task you listed under Respond in the Risk Management section on page 111.
4. Record any of your observations in the Risk Journal.

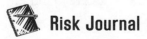

Risk Journal

7

"use me"

This week's session is based on chapter 15, "Suit Up and Show Up," and chapter 16, "Yes, You," in Risk.

When I daydream about some daring adventure or heroic act I might perform, I often imagine myself dressed in camo or black and on a mission for the Special Forces of the U.S. armed forces.

Oh, I love these guys—the Navy SEALs, the Army Rangers, the Delta Force. What would it be like to endure all that training and then be deployed on a stealth mission that demands skill and guts? And what if you or I were asked to be a mission leader? What a test for any man!

Well, if you have had some dreams like that, I have good news. Every God's man is part of the greatest special forces team ever called into battle. Refined skills and raw bravery are required. And there are huge risks. Are you ready for a mission? Come on—lace up your boots. Our Commander is ready to brief us.

Risk Analysis

We God's men have a lot to learn from the warriors in the Special Forces.

> If a soldier is caught behind enemy lines, for example, these guys get the call. If a terrorist cell is discovered and poses a lethal threat to the safety and security of our country, these men in black are called in. If reconnaissance is needed on the enemy and detection is not an option, these guys are camouflaged and dropped in from the stratosphere and *left there* for long periods. Special needs require special missions by special men trained and equipped to do what's necessary under pressure to achieve their country's objectives. They have a mission, and behind their mission is a cause—usually freedom for someone or something.
>
> The spirit of these warriors is like the spirit of God's men. In fact, when God finds a man who is passionate for His purposes, trained in the Word, filled with the Spirit, humble in heart, He will send that man into situations unsuited for others. The men, like the missions, are different, even odd, but they are custom-trained for these jobs—jobs only they can do.

1. Think of some of God's men in Scripture—Abraham, Noah, Joseph, Moses, David, Nehemiah, the disciples, Stephen, Paul, Timothy—and, of course, Jesus. What qualities do you see in these guys that would qualify them for the Special Forces?

2. What's your reaction to the fact that the greater your spiritual maturity as a man of God, the tougher might be your special assignments?

📖 The original God-Man knew why He was here, and we, under His leadership, should think the same when it comes to our mission on earth. On earth, Jesus was focused and mindful that the mission window was closing and He needed to seize the moment. More important, He wanted His men to see the urgent need to fulfill *their* mission even as He was committed to His own. 📖

3. What do you consider your mission on earth to be?

4. What might be the outcome if you do not complete the mission God has assigned to you?

I often wonder how many missions God has sent His men into that were left unfinished because of an inability see the situation clearly. How many windows of opportunity have been missed? Let's be honest, that should scare the snot out of every God's man called to serve and lead. I never want my men at Saddleback to miss their mission windows or relax when they need to be focused. I tell them they have to look at themselves as God's special forces, divinely inserted, specifically tasked, and spiritually equipped to redeem the lost causes from the talons of the Enemy. They need to walk into, not out of, situations that require any kind of leadership.

5. Can you recall any instances in your life where you missed a window of opportunity to accomplish some specific task for God and His kingdom?

6. Are you facing some situations now where God might want you to deploy and accomplish some objective for Him? What are they and what might you do?

Wondrously stunned God's men have said to me, "If you'd have asked me ten years ago if I'd be doing this [kind of work for the Lord], I would've said you were crazy or something real close."

7. Can you identify with the previous thought that you have come a long way in your Christian journey? List some examples.

The apostle Paul would have made an outstanding Delta Force commando. He thought like one, but more important, he lived like one. He didn't live for man but for the Supreme Commander. "The most important thing is that I complete my mission, the work that the Lord Jesus gave me—to tell people the Good News about God's grace" (Acts 20:24, NCV). This is how God's man thinks. He accepts assignments, and he finishes them. Big or small, significant or trivial, they are his responsibility to execute.

To think like this requires a different perspective toward yourself, toward life, and toward your real day-to-day purpose. You have to have different objectives than the men around you. You have to have eternal objectives. You have to consider the spiritual stakes of inaction.

8. To what extent is "tell[ing] people the Good News about God's grace" a part of the mission objective of every God's man?

9. How would you say your personal goals and objectives differ from those of many men you know?

📖 The message is simple: accept your assignments on earth, complete them, and become a true God's man. Remember the giver of the assignment, remember His words, and remember that He lives in you. To His Father He prayed, "I have brought you glory on earth by completing the work you gave me to do" (John 17:4).

Accomplish the work He has given you. Everything else is a diversion. 📖

10. Jesus had to give His very life to complete His mission on earth. In what aspects of your mission for Christ and His kingdom do you feel you are having to sacrifice huge parts of your life?

Two Mighty Words

I like to say, "Willing men inspire fear." Not fear in others, but fear in the devil. If you want to get the Enemy and his cohorts in a sweat, just say these two words to God every day: "Use me."

That's pretty much what Isaiah the prophet said: "Then I heard the voice of the Lord saying, 'Whom shall I send? And who will go for us?' And I said, 'Here am I. Send me!' " (Isaiah 6:8).

"Use me." Two little words—a verb and a pronoun. What's the big deal, you say? Put the two together, speak them sincerely to God, and mean it. In the natural realm, it may seem insignificant. But in the spiritual world there are huge repercussions.

- It means a soldier has been added—a marine, ready to be the "first to fight" for souls.
- It means God's man gets promoted from a bit player to the starting lineup.
- It means conversations about Christ and countless eternal consequences start spinning out into solid patterns.
- It means salvation, connection, and transformation of lives.
- It means forgiveness and healing.
- It means the game has changed forever.
- It means a warrior has been born and the gates of hell will not prevail against him.
- It means God's man has joined the ultimate battle line—the one of true consequence, the one that determines eternal destinies.
- It means a new asset is in play for the Enemy to contend with.

1. If you are a parent, boss, teacher, volunteer coach, or in any type of authority over others, describe your reactions when your child (or employee or student or team member) immediately obeys you—with a smile and a good attitude.

2. Why do you think our willing obedience is so important and gratifying to God?

📖 Willingness on the part of God's man to share the gospel is weapons-grade plutonium in spiritual warfare—the final ingredient that makes a nuclear impact possible. How is that, you say? Simple: telling someone else about the Lord requires humility and faith, the two most powerful agents of spiritual conductivity. 📖

3. Why would humility and faith be the "two most powerful agents" of spiritual vitality and strength? (Food for thought? Check out Proverbs 22:4; Matthew 17:20, 18:4; Mark 9:23; Philippians 3:9; Hebrews 11:6; James 4:10; and 1 Peter 5:5–6.)

📖 God's man can choose to experience the power of God by deciding to share his faith. Jesus put it this way to His guys: "You will receive power when the Holy Spirit comes on you; and you will be my witnesses in Jerusalem, and in all Judea and Samaria, and to the ends of the earth" (Acts 1:8). Whoa! Now that's a blast zone.

The only thing the boys were waiting for now was the ignition switch of the

Holy Spirit. It came at Pentecost where they all went nuclear, boldly sharing the gospel without fear (note: for the full picture read Acts 2–4 and take a look at the promise fulfilled). The point to ponder is this: the power is given and the power is experienced by God's man when he opens his mouth for the King.

4. What does it mean, in the context of sharing the gospel, to be a witness?

5. Have you experienced the power of God in a unique way when sharing the gospel or talking about spiritual matters with another person? Jot down the details.

God Power

The apostle Paul ignited this insight into how God's man experiences the release of God's power in and through him: "When I came to you, brothers, I did not come with eloquence or superior wisdom as I proclaimed to you the testimony about God. For I resolved to know nothing while I was with you except Jesus Christ and him crucified. I came to you in weakness and fear, and with much trembling. My message and my preaching were not with wise and persuasive words, but with a demonstration of the Spirit's power, so that your faith might not rest on men's wisdom, but on God's power" (1 Corinthians 2:1–5). He showed up. He was willing to open his mouth. And the rest was on God.

The point to ponder here is this: for God's man, intellectual knowledge is not the issue. "I don't know enough" is no longer in play. In fact, the less we claim to know, the more raw and honest the message, the more power flows through us. 🕮

1. Why do you think it's important that the validity of the gospel "not rest on men's wisdom, but on God's power"?

2. Sometimes, new believers are some of the more effective communicators of the gospel. Why do you think that's true?

🕮 Few men I work with are naturally aggressive in sharing their faith. Most of us need to train up and into spiritual confidence first. We have to *own* it.

The key to developing God's purpose for evangelism starts here. We must be convinced that this is His priority for our lives. God commands that we go and make disciples (see Matthew 28:18–20). Next, we need to pray for opportunities and be mindful that God will layer us into situations—some obvious and some not so obvious—that call us to share our testimony and the gospel on His time. Last, we are to proactively pursue, encourage, and sharpen each other in witnessing. 📖

3. We need to be bold in sharing the gospel, but what role do you feel timing plays in effectively witnessing for Christ?

4. Why is it so important to be in tune with the Holy Spirit to effectively communicate the gospel?

📖 Whether you are a veteran or just now blasting off toward the challenge, praying the following prayer on a regular basis will help form your heart for reaching others for Christ.

Lord Jesus, thank You for reaching out to me. I want to be God's man in reaching others with the good news of Your great love. I ask You to open my heart to people's eternal condition and future, to open my ears to hear the needs around me and meet them, to lead me to the specific people You want me to talk to, to open the doors and opportunities for me to share with them, to open my mouth to share clearly, sincerely, and openly about how You came into my life and changed me. Thank You that I have what I ask because I ask according to Your will. In the name of Jesus I pray, Amen.

If you prayed that and meant it, watch out. You've just said to God: "Use me." He's going to bring those people. It's game-on time for the kingdom!

Risk Management

Remember

I am not ashamed of the gospel, because it is the power of God for the salvation of everyone who believes. (Romans 1:16)

Special Note

When God answers your prayer and uses you to touch someone for Christ, please tell me so I can celebrate with you. E-mail your story to kennyl@everymanministries.com. And if you would like to get ahold of resources that will help you share your faith, log on to www.everymanministries.com and click the *Risk* book icon on the home page.

Reflect

Being "not ashamed" is where you and I need to be intellectually, emotionally, and spiritually when it comes to sharing our faith. Add a bit of Special Forces bravery. Then just do it—that's the faith part. We won't become confident on our mission assignments until we get some experience. The results will come, because this is what God wants. My point: risk sharing your faith—even once. Then the next time won't feel so strange. And the next time, and so on.

1. Why is the gospel so powerful?

2. Understanding what the gospel has done for you and can do for others, would it not make sense to be proud of the gospel? Do you have any reservations about enthusiastically and proudly sharing the good news with others? If so, what are they? What are you going to do about it?

Respond

If you have not done so before, write out your personal testimony. Although you may not use your testimony verbatim with someone else, the exercise of stating specifically what God has done for you and what you believe about your Christian faith will encourage you. It may also reveal any areas of question or doubt. Be prepared to read your written testimony to your accountability partner. (If you have written your testimony before, is it time for a new release of your witness software?)

Risk Assessment (Man to Man)

1. Catch up with each other. Take turns reading your personal testimony to each other. Share constructive comments that might result in improvements.
2. Close in prayer. Be sure to pray specifically for each other's needs. Also pray for the people with whom you are sharing the gospel.

Risk and Reward (Small Group Discussion)

1. Why do you agree or disagree with the statement from *Risk,* "Crises demand good leadership or else people suffer"?
2. There are a lot of situations where someone needs to step up and provide unselfish, sacrificial leadership. Fear about the consequences needs to be swallowed up by trust in God. Here are some situations that require some Special Forces–type courage. Pick out a few to discuss.
   - A married co-worker tells you he's about to have an affair.
   - You are on a plane with a total stranger who needs to consider the gospel over a guru.
   - Your wife asks you if she can trim giving to the church one month so that she can put in the new floor.
   - Your brother-in-law has an alcohol problem and his family is suffering.
   - Your friend is suicidal and he calls to tell *you.*
   - A family member is dying who has not professed Christ as Savior.
   - Bitterness is destroying a family relationship.
   - You have vision for a project in the world that will honor God.
   - You have the means and have been approached to fund a ministry project.
   - There is a felt need in your community, and you have concrete ideas about how to meet it.
   - Your church is calling for people to participate in a relief effort, and they need a leader.
   - You see that the guys in your couples group need to connect outside the group in a men's setting to talk about men's stuff.
3. What comments or actions by others sap your courage the most when you are seeking to do something strategic or risky for God?
4. Trade some of your stories about sharing the gospel—both the successes and the apparent failures.

5. Can there really be a failure if you obediently share the good news with another person?
6. There has long been a debate over the relative merits of verbal witnessing in sharing the gospel versus lifestyle evangelism. Why do you think one of these techniques is more effective than the other? Is there a time for both? Both at once?
7. There comes a point where the training is done. It's time to go on the mission. How can we, as God's men, make sure we leave the rifle range and head into the battle of sharing the gospel with the lost?

Risk Behavior

Here's what needs to happen before the next small group meeting:

1. Complete your personal study of session 8, which includes reading chapter 17 in *Risk.*
2. Meet with your accountability partner.
3. Accomplish the Risk task you listed under Respond in the Risk Management section on page 130.
4. Record any of your observations in the Risk Journal.

Risk Journal

____

____

8

risk it all

This week's session is based on chapter 17, "Bet It All," in Risk.

This is it—the last session in our journey to get better at risking it all for the only cause that really matters.

In *Risk* I told the story of Mohammed Odeh Al-Rehaief, the Iraqi who risked everything to help win the freedom of a prisoner of war, the wounded American soldier, Jessica Lynch. Al-Rehaief is an iron-clad warrior. He even endured the horror of losing one eye while selflessly trying to help a person he'd never met.

I want to be that kind of God's man—willing to bet it all for the glory of God and the advancement of His kingdom. In this final chapter we will dissect why Al-Rehaief is such a hero and how his story can instruct us in living a life of risk.

Risk Analysis

In Al-Rehaief we learn not just about a great man who did a great thing, we see a parable of how men are moved beyond self-preservation to greatness. We see the anatomy of the thoughts and actions of a true hero.

- *He reciprocated with risk.* He saw men and women risking their lives for him and felt a responsibility to risk back. *That* was the right thing to do. *He made it personal.*
- *He reacted right away.* He felt a deep gratitude when he looked at Jessica Lynch. He let it hit him emotionally. It was an emotional reaction at first. Then he let it move from his heart *past his head* and to his behavior in *real time.* That is, in time to help. *He didn't overthink it.*
- *He released the outcomes.* He acted on principle and did not require guaranteed outcomes. Death. Life. Success. Failure. *He was going regardless.*
- *He remembered his duty.* He did not excuse himself from his responsibility to act. His inner constitution prevailed over fears or feelings that might amend or bend it. *He lived out his values.*
- *He ran into the dark.* He did not let the unknowns stop him. He leapt, not knowing if a net would appear. He could not see where his risk was going to take him. *He discovered the way one step at a time.*
- *He resisted retreat.* He showed his commitment by going *back* twice. He exposed himself repeatedly and at a higher chance of death. *He did not look for a back door so he could back off.*
- *He relied on a higher purpose.* He connected helping a woman live to helping the cause of liberty in his own life and for his people. These purposes provided courage and confidence to risk it all. They dignified and justified his efforts. *He fortified and strengthened his resolve by uniting his actions to a greater cause.*

1. What might have happened if Al-Rehaief had taken the opposite course and ignored Jessica Lynch—not just to her but to America and the war effort?

2. What can be the results when one of God's soldiers turns away from the path of selfless sacrifice?

3. On a daily basis, what evidence do you encounter that every follower of Jesus is engaged in spiritual combat?

The Risk Taker Hall of Fame

Taking risks for God leads to a richer relationship with Him. More important, when we push the envelope of His promises, we get to personally see His purposes worked out in the world.

Think Abraham's emergency relocation process. Think Joshua and the march-and-blow strategy for Jericho. Think Noah's shipping order. Think of Joshua getting a million people to the other side of the river, only to start multiple wars based on a promise. Think of David teeing off on Goliath. Think Elijah calling out the prophets of Baal. Think Daniel refusing steak and asking for veggies. Think Stephen before the Sanhedrin. Think Jesus in the Garden of Gethsemane. Think [your name here] plus [risk issue].

Every guy was God's man. Every guy was tested. Every man stood alone. Every man risked trusting God and prevailed.

1. Of all these Bible characters, with which one do you identify the most—the guy about whom you say to yourself, *I understand him—he reminds me of me.* Why do you feel this way?

2. These Bible heroes were risk takers. What does that fact reveal about the qualities God is looking for in the men He wants to use?

3. Most of these Bible saints also had personal flaws. How does that fact encourage you to be a risk taker?

📖 These are the big hitters, the Hall of Famers, the recognized risk takers. But it would be a mistake to think that slaying a giant, crossing a river, being killed as a martyr, or calling down fire is all that garners God's attention. The Bible makes it clear that any decision to put God's agenda ahead of yours, ahead of money, ahead of feelings, titles, and desires pleases God.

The Word ahead of the world. The gospel ahead of gurus. Self-sacrifice over selfishness. Relationships over busyness. These are also the risks that are recognized, recorded, and rewarded by God. The Bible says that any loss related to these risks taken for Him and His purposes—whether literal, emotional, relational, circumstantial, financial, or whatever-al—will be compensated in full by God. 📖

4. What are some of the benefits of obedience and risk taking for God here on earth? (For clues, read Exodus 19:5; Deuteronomy 5:29; 1 Kings 3:14; James 1:25; and many more.)

5. What are the rewards in heaven? (For clues, read 1 Corinthians 9:25; 2 Timothy 4:8; James 1:12; 1 Peter 5:4; and many more.)

📖 Jesus made sure to get His guys ready for living a life shaped by risk early in the game.

"Blessed are you who are poor, for yours is the kingdom of God. Blessed are you who hunger now, for you will be satisfied. Blessed are you who weep now, for you will laugh. Blessed are you when men hate you, when they exclude you and insult you and reject your name as evil, because of the Son of Man. Rejoice in that day and leap for joy, because great is your reward in heaven" (Luke 6:20–23).

Living as God's men would involve sacrifice. But Jesus wanted to make triple-dog sure that His guys had His official guarantee: the score would be settled, and they would be elated at the return. The investment had to be made *now;* everything would be left on the field. They would be called to risk putting their entire lives in play for the kingdom.

And the rewards would all come to them, some on earth but mostly in heaven. Every God's man is called to arrange his life and make a choice that spiritual safety is no longer an option. 📖

6. It seems counterintuitive to think that being poor, hungry, weepy, and hated is blessed. Jesus is getting at something that does not make too much sense from a normal human perspective. How do you believe the beatitudes relate to your life?

7. How do you respond to the idea that the majority of your reward for serving God will not be received until you are in heaven?

📖 The spiritually safe life is ultimately the most dangerous of all. How dangerous? Paul put it to the Corinthians this way: if you risk nothing for your faith on earth, you waste your grace.

"By the grace God has given me, I laid a foundation as an expert builder, and someone else is building on it. But each one should be careful how he builds. For no one can lay any foundation other than the one already laid, which is Jesus Christ. If any man builds on this foundation using gold, silver, costly stones, wood, hay or straw, his work will be shown for what it is, because the Day will bring it to light. It will be revealed with fire, and the fire will test the quality of each man's work. If what he has built survives, he will receive his reward. If it is burned up, he will suffer loss; he himself will be saved, but only as one escaping through the flames." (1 Corinthians 3:10–15). 📖

8. Why is it so important to build your life on the right foundation?

9. What do you think Paul means by using "gold, silver, costly stones" in a foundation?

10. What might "wood, hay or straw" represent?

The One Thing: Follow Jesus

> Keep your eyes on *Jesus* who both began and finished this race we're in. Study how he did it. Because he never lost sight of where he was headed—that exhilarating finish in and with God—he could put up with anything along the way: cross, shame, whatever. And now he's *there,* in the place of honor, right alongside God. When you find yourselves flagging in your faith, go over that story again, item by item, that long litany of hostility he plowed through. *That* will shoot adrenaline into your souls! (Hebrews 12:2–3, MSG)

📖 We can't look up at the Man on the cross and lose in our quest to throw spiritual caution and fear to the wind. Instead we can only be strengthened in our resolve to risk progressively more and more. In fact, the longer we look at

Him up there, the more dangerous we become for the kingdom. We join the ranks of men who saw Him from a distance and risked, men who walked with Him up close, and men who through the centuries endangered others with kingdom-splitting conviction.

If you are to bet it all, study the Man who risked it all. 📖

1. We have learned a great deal about the cost of discipleship in this workbook. Ultimately, though, it all comes down to knowing Jesus, loving Jesus, obeying Jesus, risking it all for Jesus. As this study nears an end, what specific qualities about you accurately describe your devotion to Christ?

📖 Every risk we take for Him, He earned and then some. We will never be able to pay Him back. But we can show our gratitude by remembering the greatest risk ever taken and responding gratefully with some risk taking of our own. He will show us His stripes one day—the scars. The ones on His body that healed us and saved us. He will show us because scars tell stories. Scars prove your story. Scars remind. Scars show the cost. Scars motivate. Scars inspire. And scars are beautiful.

Scars tell you that a Man was not playing it safe.

And that Man lives in you. 📖

Risk Management

Remember

> Since we are surrounded by such a great cloud of witnesses, let us throw off everything that hinders and the sin that so easily entangles, and let us run with perseverance the race marked out for us. Let us fix our eyes on Jesus, the author and perfecter of our faith, who for the joy set before him endured the cross, scorning its shame, and sat down at the right hand of the throne of God. (Hebrews 12:1–2)

Reflect

1. Is there anything that "hinders" or "so easily entangles" you that needs to be eradicated so that you can run your race well for Christ? He's waiting to take care of things—ask Him now!

2. As best as you understand it now, what is the race God has set before you? (Run it well, my brother!)

Respond

This study is ending, but your journey continues. Spend a few minutes paging through this workbook. List here the important ideas, scriptures, insights, and commitments you do not want to forget.

1.

2.

3.

4.

5.

6.

7.

8.

 Risk Assessment (Man to Man)

This is the last time you need to get together—as part of this study. But why stop now? In only a few weeks, you have already tasted the first sips of the good wine of an authentic man-to-man accountability relationship.

1. Once again review the last week and share what God has been up to in your lives. Place your needs before the Lord, and thank Him for His goodness and faithfulness.
2. If you plan to continue as accountability partners, firm up details as to when and where you will meet. Also, do you plan to study a book of the Bible or a Christian book? Make some decisions on what is next.
3. Finish with prayer.

 Risk and Reward (Small Group Discussion)

1. Roger Bannister broke a barrier some thought would never be broken—the four-minute mile. When he reflected on his titanic athletic achievement, he said, "The man who can drive himself further once the pain starts is the man who will win." Do you agree or disagree with what Bannister said? Is pain that important in growing and achieving success?
2. Many men spend a lot of time and effort investing in earthly things. What role should the activities and things of this life play for a man following God?
3. What rewards have you experienced here on earth for following and obeying the Lord Jesus?
4. In *Risk* we read: "The good energy, the big choices, the core relationships, and the productive capacities are our precious offerings we risk placing in God's hands for His multiplication. The critical mistake so many make is carving out

only a small part of their life portfolio for Him, investing in other things that produce no return." What would be some examples of investments a man might make that will not produce a return in the end?

5. Ultimately, all of us are betting our lives on the trustworthiness of Jesus. Why would you say it's a safe risk to lay it all down for Him?
6. As this study on risk concludes, what will be the most threatening temptations and challenges to living as a God's man until Christ returns or we each head home?

Risk Behavior

There's no assignment now except to be a risk taker for God. Here's a parting thought:

> Only those who risk going too far can possibly find out how far they can go.
> —T. S. Eliot

And, one more time, this is a scripture you need to live and breathe:

> Since we are surrounded by such a great cloud of witnesses, let us throw off everything that hinders and the sin that so easily entangles, and let us run with perseverance the race marked out for us. Let us fix our eyes on Jesus, the author and perfecter of our faith, who for the joy set before him endured the cross, scorning its shame, and sat down at the right hand of the throne of God. (Hebrews 12:1–2)

Go get 'em.

See you on the field.

Risk Journal